Cambridge El

Elements in Political E
edited by
David Stasavage
New York University

A MORAL POLITICAL ECONOMY: PRESENT, PAST, AND FUTURE

Federica Carugati
King's College London

Margaret Levi
Stanford University

CAMBRIDGE
UNIVERSITY PRESS

CAMBRIDGE
UNIVERSITY PRESS

University Printing House, Cambridge CB2 8BS, United Kingdom

One Liberty Plaza, 20th Floor, New York, NY 10006, USA

477 Williamstown Road, Port Melbourne, VIC 3207, Australia

314–321, 3rd Floor, Plot 3, Splendor Forum, Jasola District Centre,
New Delhi – 110025, India

79 Anson Road, #06–04/06, Singapore 079906

Cambridge University Press is part of the University of Cambridge.

It furthers the University's mission by disseminating knowledge in the pursuit of
education, learning, and research at the highest international levels of excellence.

www.cambridge.org
Information on this title: www.cambridge.org/9781108819398
DOI: 10.1017/9781108872942

© Federica Carugati and Margaret Levi 2021

First published 2021

A catalogue record for this publication is available from the British Library.

ISBN 978-1-108-81939-8 Paperback
ISSN 2398-4031 (online)
ISSN 2514-3816 (print)

A Moral Political Economy: Present, Past, and Future

Elements in Political Economy

DOI: 10.1017/9781108872942
First published online: May 2021

Federica Carugati
King's College London

Margaret Levi
Stanford University

Author for correspondence: Margaret Levi, mlevi@stanford.edu

Abstract: Economies – and the government institutions that support them – reflect a moral and political choice, a choice we can make and remake. Since the dawn of industrialization and democratization in the late eighteenth century, there has been a succession of political economic frameworks, reflecting changes in technology, knowledge, trade, global connections, political power, and the expansion of citizenship. The challenges of today reveal the need for a new moral political economy that recognizes the politics in political economy. It also requires the redesign of our social, economic, and governing institutions based on assumptions about humans as social beings rather than narrow self-serving individualists. This Element makes some progress toward building a new moral political economy by offering both a theory of change and some principles for institutional (re)design.

Keywords: Political economy, moral economy, institutions, neo-liberalism, neo-classical economics, behavior, cooperation, governance, relational equality, democratic capabilities, communities of fate, participation.

ISBNs: 9781108819398 (PB), 9781108872942 (OC)
ISSNs: 2398-4031 (online), 2514-3816 (print)

Contents

1 Toward a New Moral Political Economy

Economies – and the government institutions that support them – reflect a moral and political choice, a choice we can make and remake. Since the dawn of industrialization and democratization in the late eighteenth century, there has been a succession of political economic frameworks, reflecting changes in technology, knowledge, trade, global connections, political power, and the expansion of citizenship.

The challenges of today reveal the need for a new moral political economy. COVID-19 and the Black Lives Matter movement are reshaping our model of the world and creating new opportunities to reform laws and policies. The global pandemic exposed how poorly some of our most basic structures are serving us. The reignited racial justice movement calls out the biases and prejudices enshrined within our agencies, our practices, and ourselves.

Democracy itself is embattled due to the combination of polarization, disinformation, gridlock, poor leadership, and outmoded design principles. The belief is waning that the market can solve all problems. The temporary reduction in pollution resulting from shelter-in-place rules is making even more apparent the human contribution to the existential crisis of climate change. Inequality of agency and power is rising with inequality of income. In principle, our societies have the capacity to feed, house, and provide health care to all, yet far too many are hungry, homeless, or suffering from preventable illness and death.

Indicators of the fraying of the current political economic framework, popularly called neoliberalism,[1] began to emerge well before 2020. In part, neoliberalism is floundering because of the transformations in the economy and technologies on which it was based. In part, it is floundering because of its failures.

For decades, manufacturing has been declining as the engine of the economy in many industrialized countries. This has led to a relocation of jobs and new educational and training requirements for the jobs that are available. One additional consequence is the undermining of unions, an important mechanism of worker voice and power. The cumulative effects are new anxieties among the populace, new demands on the social insurance system, and new political coalitions (Collier 2018).

---

[1] This term has been adopted widely. It is a contested term that fails to convey the full complexity of the ideas and practices embodied in the current political economic framework. Supply-side economics, the Chicago School, many varieties of post-Keynes Keynesianism, and almost all of neoclassical economics seem to be covered by the term. We adopt it here because of its general usage and familiarity.

Simultaneously, digital technology magnifies our capacity to communicate, but it also changes how we think, how we read, how we view the world. While extending access to information and knowledge, it poses new challenges to our conceptions of privacy, attention, good information, corporate power, state capacity, and our sense of self and others. Machine learning and more sophisticated algorithms raise concerns about fairness, human autonomy, and the future of work.

The Great Recession of 2008 and how governments dealt with blameworthy financial institutions and failed to deal adequately with peoples' distress was for many a turning point. The subsequent resurgence of populism led to protests on the street and votes for significant changes in leadership and policy. The palpable and general discontent with the liberal consensus on how globalization has evolved is one source of the unraveling of support for the status quo, but equally important is citizen dissatisfaction with public education, social insurance, retraining, health care, and other expected government services. Contestation of values and fears about the disappearance of cherished ways of life (Cramer 2016; Hochschild 2016) further contribute to polarization and the unraveling of the social cohesion and social compacts that helped sustain the system.

Yet, dissatisfaction with the status quo has for long coexisted with a widespread belief in its immutability. Today, as in the past, economic and political structures are perceived as given, natural, and stable. Indeed, the major achievement of neoliberalism – and all political economic frameworks before it – is to make normative prescriptions seem like descriptive statements of the natural behavior of people, governments, and organizations. A set of structures, crafted by some humans to fit one era, become understood as timeless and universal.

This is a parlor trick. Since at least the end of the eighteenth century, capitalist political economic frameworks – which are the focus of this Element – have evolved, acquiring new organizational and ownership forms for production and finance, as technologies and exploitative opportunities changed. Capitalist democracies extended the franchise and altered their institutional arrangements and practices many times over the last two centuries. Revised governmental and economic structures for social insurance, financial stabilization, health and welfare protections, and infrastructure development arose in the twentieth century in the wake of the World Wars and the Great Depression.

As we discuss in Section 2, neoliberalism hasn't always been the dominant political economic framework. However, the obliteration of the illusion that neoliberalism represents ultimately depends on its failure to meet contemporary needs and demands. The same happened with previous frameworks: stagflation helped bring down Keynesianism; government and corporate incapacity in the face of the pandemic, unemployment, hunger, climate change, and racial injustice will likely topple its successor. The world has altered, and we must adapt. We are now living in a "white water world," where change is constant and new forms of flexible learning and action are increasingly necessary (Pendleton-Jullian and Brown 2018). The question is where we go next.

We have the opportunity now to remake our political economies to promote more equitable and general well-being for humans and the environment. We need to move beyond economic growth as a societal end and as a metric. We need to improve the capacity of democratic government to respond to the losers of neoliberalism, while checking the powerful and mitigating the harms they created. This means strengthening our embattled democracies by reaffirming fundamental democratic values, including voice and political equality. And it requires us to provide a new basis for social cohesion and inclusiveness.

Our argument for building a new political economy is rooted in the notion of "expanded communities of fate" (Ahlquist and Levi 2013; Levi 2020).[2] An expanded community of fate extends beyond the groups to which one most naturally belongs. The recognition of belonging to a larger and inclusive community of fate can motivate us to act in solidarity with strangers and with peoples who can never directly reciprocate. Its members are willing to make sacrifices on behalf of those with whom they believe their destinies, and their descendants' destinies, are entwined.

The notion of community of fate echoes similar concepts used throughout the twentieth century by those seeking social justice. So, for Martin Luther King, Jr., "we are caught in an inescapable network of mutuality, tied in a single garment of destiny. Whatever affects one directly, affects all indirectly" (King 1964). Similarly, the labor movement – the Knights of Labor, International Workers of the World (IWW), and the International Longshore and Warehouse Workers (ILWU) – adopted as their motto "An injury to one is an injury to all." A related but distinctive concept is "linked fate" in which one's life chances are entwined with a group (Dawson 1994; Simien 2005).[3]

---

[2] Ahlquist and Levi were not the first to use the term "community of fate." It has several lineages, but a disturbing variant was the Nazi usage of *Schicksalsgemeinschaft* to evoke an exclusive, racist, nationalist community. When President Obama and his speechwriter discovered this historical usage, they decided to take it out of a speech Obama was soon to deliver (Rhodes 2019; Obama 2020). Levi's experience in Germany is that the term can be used to denote an inclusive or exclusive community (see, e.g., Kundanini 2018), as Ahlquist and Levi make clear (2013, 277). It is one of the reasons that they – and we in this book – emphasize an *expanded* and *inclusive* community of fate.

[3] Generally, this concept refers only to those in one's ethnic or racial group but can embrace those in other racial and ethnic groups perceived as undergoing similar discrimination (Craig and Richeson 2012; Cox 2019).

In this Element, we articulate how we can begin to design an expanded community of fate as a base for a new, more inclusive, moral political economy.

The Components of a New Moral Political Economic Framework

Political economy refers to the frameworks that have always organized human societies. The word "framework" stresses the importance of the rules and institutions that govern and guide our choices and actions. Our focus in this Element is on the rules and institutions that have evolved since the late eighteenth-century emergence of capitalist democracies. As we will elaborate in Section 2, the early frameworks were grounded in a comprehensive understanding of economies, governments, societies, and their moral foundations. By the twentieth century it was economics alone that dominated analysis.

This Element aims to rescue the politics in *political* economy and to make explicit the underlying *moral* dimension of any political economy. "Politics" here refers to both the means by which a society determines its policies and laws and the configuration of power, that is, who has the capacity to effect or block change. "Moral" refers to the values that inform the framework itself as well as the actions undertaken by governments, economic actors, and citizens in keeping with the framework. The term "moral political economy" accentuates how economies are a moral and political choice and how their definitions of fairness structure both policy and citizen responses to their situation.

Moral economy (Polanyi 1957; for a history of the concept see Rogan 2017) has roots in the extra-market reciprocal rights and obligations between landlords and peasants. During the industrial era, the term referred to the obligations of society to provide for the welfare of the population, particularly those displaced or impoverished. A moral economy also entitles citizens to resist when they believe that there are violations of their rights or due. Sometimes they mobilize and sometimes they engage in forms of noncompliance that are the weapons of the weak (Scott 1985). Catalysts to resistance are not only material changes in peoples' status quo but also – and sometimes in contradistinction to their narrow interests – changes to what they perceive as violations of norms of fairness and justice, of wounds to their dignity, and of failure to recognize the worth of their cultures.

All political economies are moral in our sense. However, liberal political economies tolerate multiple conceptions and contestations over what constitutes the good; there is no single moral code (Rawls 1993; Anderson 1999, 329–31). What values receive preeminence vary over time and place. Neoliberalism, the moral political economy that we hope to replace, emphasizes freedom and liberty in the form of noninterference, particularly by government on business and, to a lesser extent, on individuals. But there are other conceptions of freedom and liberty and other values that also deserve consideration, as we shall soon see.

A moral political economic framework, then, combines the rules that structure economic and political behavior, as well as the norms, values, and goals on which the structure is built. The rules determine the reciprocal rights and obligations that link populations, governments, corporations, and all the other various organizations that make up the society. Its norms, values, and goals regulate what constitutes legitimate behavior (Levi 2019).

Theory of Change

Before we delve deeper into the rules and institutions of a new moral political economy, we must first lay out our theory of change. What makes us think this is an opportune moment? And how do we get from here to where we want to go?

Capitalist political economies hold out the promise of economic growth and innovation that will improve the standard of living and the well-being of the general population. They evolve with changes in technology, demography, and economic organization and in response to depressions and wars. But these factors, important as they are, are not solely responsible for shifts in political economic frameworks. Perhaps even more fundamental is the contestation over power. When the status quo is robust, vested interests shape policy to benefit them and those on whom the maintenance of their power depends. If the system begins to ossify and inhibit economic growth, competition arises.

With the emergence of each set of powerful economic elites comes demands on the political economy to ensure it serves their interests better. If there is also a deterioration of general well-being, accompanied by public outcries and mass mobilization, the window is opened wide to new policies, practices, and even alternative whole political economic frameworks. The moment may also be ripe for revisions of the social contract and to reconsideration of the values that should undergird the system.

Contestation over policy has always existed, but it now encompasses a far wider and varied set of actors. The evolution of democracy in the nineteenth and twentieth centuries has given more competitors voice and clout. Powerful economic interests, vying to become or remain the capitalist mandarins, realized that their ability to protect themselves required enhancing the well-being of a significant proportion of the population (Boix 2003; Acemoglu and Robinson 2006; Ansell and Samuels 2010; Iversen and Soskice 2019). Expression of pent-up demand and frustration through elections and popular mobilization are often the precipitants to this realization.

While public and publicized traumas make people sit up and take notice that the system is badly awry, it is the development of a widespread movement for change that can affect the balance of power in a political economy. The murder of George Floyd, captured on video and circulated worldwide, is a recent instance of popular mobilization in response to injustice. But the past abounds with other examples, among them the Triangle Shirt Waist Factory Fire in New York City in 1911 or the Rana Plaza collapse in Bangladesh in 2013. Suddenly, the horrific and devalued lives of sweatshop workers became a rallying cry for reform of their working conditions by consumers, unions, and NGOs. Governments took up the cry, increasing the pressure on the international corporations who employed the workers in their supply chains (Berliner, Greenleaf, Lake, Levi, and Noveck 2015). Similarly, the tuberculosis epidemic, the Spanish flu, polio, and other diseases were catalysts for changes in public health, public education, and, indeed, in societies (Diamond 2020). Natural disasters – fires, floods, and earthquakes – can also lead to better policies and practices. So, too, can the threat of widespread social disorder or revolution (Weingast 1997; Levi, Melo, Weingast, and Zlotnick 2017). And nothing precipitates transformations of society as much as catastrophic, life-destroying wars (Olson 1982; Scheidel 2017). Physical and social infrastructure need rebuilding and rethinking in the wake of catastrophe, and so does our moral code.

Crisis and popular motivation may provide an opportunity, but actual change depends on more than a public awakening to the plight of others. Lasting reconstruction requires new ideas, effective political leadership, and structural change.

Ideas come first. Frances Perkins, the first woman to join a presidential cabinet, had well-formulated designs for new forms of social insurance and labor protections in the wake of the Great Depression. She played a pivotal role in the enactment of both Social Security and the National Labor Relations Act. Partially informed by the thinking of economist John Maynard Keynes and other leading social scientists, her ideas equally reflected experiences as a social activist and a government policy advisor.

Similarly, Nobel laureate Milton Friedman, a key progenitor of the current neoliberal framework, was among a group of economists and others who formed the Mont Pelerin Society to combat Keynesianism (Phillips-Fein 2009; Burgin 2012). An important part of their project was to come up with sound economic theories that could be translated into policies. They promoted monetarism and small and stingy government. Friedman, in particular, argued for vouchers and a negative income tax (a 1970s forerunner of universal basic income).

What Perkins and Friedman did, in their very distinctive ways, was to link their ideas to moral codes. For Perkins, it was the priority of an encompassing society that paid attention to the needy. For Friedman, it was the focus on the individual who followed the path Adam Smith prescribed: somehow, some way, the invisible hand will inevitably lead to prosperity for all.

What both Perkins and Friedman succeeded in doing was to provide the story line that enabled political leaders to become "architects of change" (Schofield 2006). Franklin Delano Roosevelt for Perkins, and Margaret Thatcher and Ronald Reagan for Friedman, engaged in what William Riker labeled *heresthetics* (Riker 1984), that is they reframed the issues in a way that overcame preexisting mental models and core beliefs and introduced an alternative perspective and suite of choices.

This model of transformative institutional change relies on ideas that change our understanding of the world.[4] But to be successful, this strategy "must do two things: (a) communicate a model of the world in which there are specific outcomes associated with differing courses of action and (b) convincingly advocate a specific outcome" (Ahlquist and Levi 2011, 8). What converted Perkins's and Friedman's ideas into practice was that their vision appealed to those with the power to effect change, whom they personally advised. But ultimately their ideas had to gain traction and legitimacy among the political and economic leadership and then with a wider audience.

FDR seized the opportunity created by the mobilization and urgent demands of the citizenry to introduce the New Deal. Prime Minister Thatcher and President Reagan, coming from a different perspective and operating in a very different era, appealed to a growing popular dissatisfaction with government bureaucracy and regulation of the economy to put forward a neoliberal agenda of deregulation and smaller government. All three heads of state were effective communicators who helped spread the ideas to a wider audience, including the general public.

The generalized acceptance of these new ideas allowed the political leadership not only to enact new policies but also to transform the very structures of government. FDR's administration expanded the reach of government to provide greater social protections and services to citizens and to create a whole new administrative apparatus and regulatory regime. The Thatcher and Reagan administrations acted to restrict federal authority over social services and protections, reduced regulations on business, and reformed government agencies, often by outsourcing their work or reducing their staff.

---

[4] There are a number of arguments that make this case. For example, see: North 1981; Denzau and North 1994; and Weingast 2005; but also, from a different perspective, Hall 1989, Weir 1989, and Blyth 2002.

The crises we are facing now provide an opportunity for the next transformation of our structures and institutions, our policies and practices, and who we include in our community of fate. We have real choices about where to go next.

Ideas

So, let us turn to our responsibility in the division of labor for effecting change. We are neither political leaders nor policymakers, so our focus will be on ideas. Our first task is to interrogate the assumptions on which the current political economic framework is built and to provide better assumptions for the next. We know far more now than we did in the past about behavior – that is, what induces people to act one way or another. Previous scientific understanding of behavior informed previous political economic frameworks, and current scientific understanding must inform the next.

Economics, the academic discipline that has dominated the construction of past political economies, has, particularly since its mathematization in the nineteenth century (see discussion in Section 2), preferred a simplified model of humans: *homo economicus*. *Homo economicus* is at the heart of neoliberalism. The rational individual is decision-maker and centerpiece, and choices are defined narrowly in terms of personal costs and benefits. From this model follow prescriptions about the expected behavior of individuals: free riding is the norm, and economic failure generally reflects personal, not structural, problems. From this model also follow prescriptions about the expected behavior of firms, governments, and the economic system itself: firms should single-mindedly maximize profit, governments are primarily to protect property rights and provide the infrastructure that the market will not, and relatively unfettered capitalism will ultimately benefit all who work and strive.

However, the premises on which such claims are based are problematic. They present a very narrow conception of human nature, motivation, and behavior. Simple aggregation of choices and actions tell us little about what people really think or will do, given the opportunity, a change in context, and a new understanding of what others believe is possible (Kuran 1995). Not only do people display systematic biases and thus make mistakes, they are also influenced by emotions, by those with whom they interact, and by societally generated norms. Narrow self-interest is an important but certainly not the only driver of action.

Any new framework must be based on the fact that humans are social beings. As Susan Fiske argues, humans are motivated to belong to a group that gives them identity and may help with survival, to create shared values and understandings, to feel that their actions have effect, to develop bases for self-esteem and self-enhancement, and to feel benevolence or trust toward others (Fiske

2003, 2010). And they are networked in complex ways that have implications for how they behave as well as consequences for the structure of influence and power in politics, economics, and social life (Jackson 2008; Ward, Stovel, and Sacks 2011; Slaughter 2017; Jackson 2019).

Indeed, the desire to connect and be part of a more integrated whole often overrides self-interest. It promotes a sense of mutualism and belonging and, therefore, trust and reciprocity. This understanding of human motivation is the basis of what Samuel Bowles and Herbert Gintis label *homo reciprocans* (Bowles and Gintis 2002) and Anne-Marie Slaughter and Hilary Cottam conceptualize as *sapiens integra* (Slaughter 2017; Cottam 2020; Cottam and Slaughter 2020). In Cottam and Slaughter's view, what people really seek is to grow their personal capabilities and that of their networks.

Substituting this more realistic and scientifically based version of human motivation for *homo economicus* is a fundamental building block for restructuring our political, economic, and social arrangements. Institutional designs based on this version must then evoke and reward caring behavior not only of the vulnerable in need of our help but also selfless actions that promote a better society. There is an evolutionary basis to this argument. Reciprocity has deep roots in our human makeup (Bowles and Gintis 2002, 2011). Care for the young and for the old is an essential process in developing the skills and the knowledge transference that ensures adults have the skills necessary to achieve their role as productive food providers (Gopnik 2020).

The claim that humans are social by nature, however, does not necessarily mean that they are always cooperative or kind to each other. Indeed, cooperation and reciprocity require institutional arrangements that can generate and sustain a commitment to act in the interest of others.

The moral vision advocated here emphasizes freedom and liberty as much as neoliberalism does. Whereas neoliberalism was largely based on negative freedom (Berlin 1970) in the form of freedom from interference, we are advocating a framework based on the freedoms essential for people to flourish within a democratic system. Freedom from want, freedom of speech, freedom from fear, and freedom to worship – the four freedoms of FDR – are necessary but not sufficient. Of equal import is the freedom to develop the capabilities that ensure people can function well within the society (Sen 1989, 1999; Nussbaum 2011). Capabilities within a democratic context demand an additional freedom, the freedom from domination (Allen 2013; Pettit 2014; Allen 2020). Democratic capabilities thus include far more than the means for survival and self-improvement. Also important are capabilities to be citizens in politics, work, and society generally. This means developing the tools needed to participate, express effective voice, mobilize, and take advantage of educational, informational, and economic opportunities.

Participation, expression, voice, and mobilization facilitate relational equality, a state of affairs in which people treat each other with respect, listen to each other, and tolerate no domination of one by another (Anderson 1993, 1999; also, see Satz and White forthcoming; Allen forthcoming). The achievement of relational equality requires that all have adequate resources so they can develop capabilities but also avoid the dependencies that produce unequal power and influence.[5]

Connectedness, cooperation, and freedom from domination are created and sustained by institutional arrangements that enable people to engage in reciprocal and prosocial behavior and to resist domination. Contemporary political philosophers recognize the need for structural supports for freedom. Elizabeth Anderson's notion of private government that is relationally equal depends on laws and rules that give workers power and dignity within corporations (Anderson 2017). Danielle Allen has long emphasized the role of law and institutions, especially education, that promote a more just polity and create bridging and bonding among citizens (Allen and Reich 2013; Allen 2016, 2020). Her argument is extended, elaborated, and made concrete in the six strategies and specific proposals in *Our Common Purpose*, the American Academy report she cochaired (Commission 2020). Other philosophers provide justifications for a range of institutional reforms and policies – from limits on the influence of money and status in politics to changes in tax, labor, and educational practices – that would promote political and economic fairness, particularly in democracies (e.g., Cohen 2001; Satz 2010; Sandel 2012; Pettit 2014; Scanlon 2018; Sandel 2020). Several argue for a more participatory politics, creating spaces for deliberation and for a wider plurality of voices (Cohen and Rogers 1995; Pettit 2014; Cohen and Fung 2021)

In Section 3, we contribute to this body of philosophical work with some practical ideas about how to create participatory spaces in today's capitalist democracies. We review a wide variety of forms of human organizations that foster cooperation and self-governance. Our account shows that such institutional arrangements exist at all scales and for many different purposes. These

---

[5] While relational equality obviously requires allocation of additional resources to build democratic capabilities, it does not necessarily imply wholesale redistribution. There is a debate among philosophers about the form of equality to pursue. We emphasize those who advocate relational equality. Anderson (2010) provides a useful summary of the debate from her perspective. The alternative is distributional equality to reduce the effects of disparities in initial fortune (e.g., Parijs 1995; Cohen 2008; Parijs and Vanderborght 2017). While all parties to the debate refer to the seminal work of John Rawls (1971, 1993), they then use him to justify different paths to justice.

cases also show that arrangements that embody important values, including voice, participation, and political equality, are still capable of effectively achieving their given objectives, such as improving the community's well-being.

From this investigation, we derive some design principles. Cooperation and self-governance work best when institutional arrangements allow members to collectively articulate and amend their governing rules and define and enforce appropriate forms of redress for those who misbehave. We find that narrow exclusivity is not a necessary condition for cooperation. Inclusive self-governance relies on features such as strong leadership, shared norms, and well-designed selection, deliberation, and decision-making mechanisms that can be built into the system.

Our inquiry suggests that we can strengthen our fraying capitalist democracies by creating institutional arrangements that return greater agency and voice to the governed and sustain relational equality. Equally important are processes for promoting learning and experimentalism to ensure the evolution of rules that take into account the diverse values of a pluralistic public.[6]

Our arguments in the next sections go some way toward building a new moral political economy. While we offer some examples of what institutional arrangements that promote democratic capabilities and relational equality might look like, our effort has many limitations and caveats. First, we must stress that the question of how to design appropriate institutions in practice is ultimately a matter of debate among the members of the polity. Such debate must be informed by a new science of governance that takes into account what we know about cooperation and self-governance, as well as the many experiments with citizen voice and engagement that are already happening around the world. The goal of this social scientific effort is to identify under what conditions participatory structures are preferable, and how they may fit within the largely representative structures of today's capitalist democracies.

Second, it is not our intention to define principles of right or ideal behavior and to enshrine those definitions in stone. Instead, our contribution is to highlight the tradeoffs involved in the moral choices that a society makes and to open up a dialogue on how to prioritize some choices and how to reconsider priorities as they change over time. While we feel it is safe to presume that everyone seeks a modicum of economic and physical security, we cannot presume their other values and their relevant tradeoffs.

---

[6] Our model of democracy is a variant of that proposed by John Dewey (1954; as elaborated in Knight and Johnson 2011; and Sabel 2012).

Based on these caveats, we view democracy as the terrain where the building process must take place. Democracy is a political system in which leaders lead with the consent of the governed. The governed express that consent through some process of voting as well as other formal and informal channels. The relatively free flow of information and debate is a hallmark of democratic political institutions but also a vulnerability. That is, the very information and debate that a democracy requires can be polluted such that the consent of the governed is rendered meaningless or, even worse, controlled by nefarious strategic actors (Farrell and Schneier 2018, 2019).

These vulnerabilities are real. However, we argue that democracy, more than any other political system yet devised, remains an engine for debate and contestation, as well as innovation and experimentation. But if the debate is left in the hands of a few experts – be they politicians, technocrats, or simply the rich – we will squander democracy's comparative advantage: its ability to harness a multiplicity of perspectives to inform decisions that affect all. Similarly, if the only space available for contestation is the street, it will become increasingly hard to channel demands for change toward productive ends.

These problems are not new, and they don't have one single answer. The concentrations of power and varieties of incorporation of new actors vary across time and place, as do the rules and laws that guide each society. Governance arrangements reflect beliefs about community membership and have real consequences for who is in and who is out of the polity. Struggles over enfranchisement, migration, religious and minority rights, and local control define the limits of citizen influence and legislative choices, but they also reflect efforts to determine the boundaries of the community of fate. Where these institutions have eroded or are failing the constituencies they are meant to serve, it is time to rebuild. But rebuilding will look different in different places.

The contemporary moment is generating demands for a renovated democracy and for transformation of existing institutions and norms. We wrote this Element to contribute to the goal of creating a better, more inclusive, and more equitable society, one that promotes the general well-being of people and the planet. Although rebuilding will ultimately look different in different places, our core contribution is to suggest that any moral political economy suited to today's capitalist democracies will have to satisfy four conditions. It must possess the means to hold the powerful accountable; to engender democratic capabilities such as effective participation and voice; to create and sustain relational equality; and to build expanded and inclusive communities of fate.

2 The Politics in Political Economy

The history of capitalist political economies is the history of economic transformation but also of new thinking about political institutions and power. Its roots are in the rise of liberalism and new forms of republicanism, in which monarchical powers are reduced and the voice of citizens and respect of their freedoms is enhanced.[7] Its roots are also in new configurations of privilege, imperialism, colonialism, and later variants of globalization, largely led by the countries of the developed North (e.g., Veblen 1953 [1912]; Keynes 1932; Slobodian 2020). Political economic theories can and have been used to justify policies that enhance the power of certain citizens and countries over that of others.

While so many contemporary writers focus on the economics within political economy, morality and politics are just as central. The field of political economy rests on more than economic models and its assumptions about how humans reason. All political economic frameworks rest on values and goals for society and make presumptions about motivations (sentiments in the classical language) and how they are evoked. Sometimes the values and goals are made explicit and sometimes not, but they are always there. This underlying moral vision informs the advocacy of institutional arrangements and policies.

Of equal import for a political economic analysis, we argue, is assessment of current power arrangements and their consequences for achieving a given vision of the good society. We agree with Eric Beinhocker that "there are two fundamental questions that economists have grappled with throughout the history of their field: how wealth is created and how wealth is allocated" (Beinhocker 2006, location 681). For political economists – if they are truly **political** economists – a key to creation and allocation of wealth is how certain key actors become dominant in the market or the state, how the two forms of power interact, and how government and law are then used to influence the creation and distribution of wealth. Why are some people winners and some losers, and what role do the structures of the political economy play in relegating them to one position or another?

Virtually all political economic theories address how government does or should affect growth, innovation, and general well-being. Government, even when limited, has a major impact on the allocation of wealth through its design and enforcement of property rights, taxation, and redistributive policies. Nobel laureate Douglass North argued "the existence of the state is essential for

---

[7] See, e.g., Kalyvas and Katznelson (2008) for a fuller discussion of the literature on and the relationship between liberalism and republicanism.

economic growth; the state, however, is the source of manmade economic decline" (North 1981, 20). Government intervention in the economy and society varies immensely over time and place, and discussion of its appropriate role – historically and in the current moment – remains the subject of ongoing debate and theorizing.

We are arguing that a political economic framework should do more than justify the particular role of government. It needs to rest on models of human motivations and rationality that are congruent with the best scientific evidence, but it must also incorporate values that promote the good of society and not just the good of a particular class or set of interests. It should identify who will be helped and who hurt by a transformation of the political economy and explicate an institutional design to redress imbalances in power. The classical political economists offered such a framework, but many subsequent economists did not. It is this encompassing approach to political economy that we hope to restore.

The classical political economists explicitly discussed the links between reason and motivations, based on the research and thinking of the day. David Hume (1975), Adam Smith (1982 [1759]), and others inspired by the Scottish Enlightenment believed that sentiments and passions affected reason, and moral commitments influenced action. These theorists, with whom our story commences, were, simultaneously, moral philosophers, modelers of the economy, and observers and analysts of politics.

The marginalists and many of the neoclassical economists who built on them were primarily economic modelers who tended to pay scant attention to considerations of values and human motivations. They also recognized few, if any, limits on rationality and adopted instead a model of perfect rationality. Finally, they largely ignored the politics of political economy. Most late nineteenth- and twentieth-century economists had, at best, a skeletal conception of politics, and their concern with power focused primarily on its excessive use – from their perspective – by government and by influential rent-seekers.

As new scientific evidence about decision-making emerged in the twentieth century, it became apparent that rationality cannot be perfect and for at least two very different reasons. First, the world is not fully knowable. Both John Maynard Keynes and Friedrich Hayek (Keynes 1936; Hayek 1974) emphasized that we make decisions in the face of uncertainty. Second, humans are cognitively constrained, subject to mistakes, illusions, and emotions. Incorporation into political economy of our cognitive limitations began, arguably, with Herbert Simon's articulation of bounded rationality (Simon 1947, 1982), followed by work on asymmetric information (e.g., Akerlof 1970; Rothschild and Stiglitz 1976; Stiglitz 1977), Amartya Sen's description of "rational fools" (Sen

1977), complexity theory (Arthur 1989, 2015), and pioneering psychological research by Amos Tversky and Daniel Kahneman on cognitive mistakes.[8]

But it is not just our knowledge of human motivation and behavior that has changed. Since the rise of capitalism, subsequent frameworks have articulated different conceptions of desirable societal goals. Nation-based economic growth has been a relatively common aim since Adam Smith. With the advent of modern democracy, there have been ongoing debates over the forms of freedom, liberty, and equity the political economy is designed to realize. However, every capitalist political economic framework claims it will raise the general standard of living and extend its benefits broadly, although not necessarily uniformly. More recently, there has been a turn to flourishing as an objective (Sen 1989, 1999; Nussbaum 2011), as well as a growing emphasis on equality and justice (e.g., Piketty 2014; Atkinson 2015).

The means for achieving such valued goals are a source of constant debate and tweaking. There is almost universal agreement that it is important to support innovation, particularly innovation in technologies, corporate organization, and political arrangements in order to better promote general well-being and economic productivity. However, if the assumptions about human behavior fail to capture what actually motivates and constrains actions, then the chosen means will be problematic in practice. If there is serious disagreement over the desired ends, then there will be political contestation over the chosen practices, policies, and agencies. If there is inattention to the role of power in enabling projected outcomes, then the model will prove empty.

Thus, a vision for the future and a theory of politics and power are necessary components of a political economic framework. Moreover, this vision and theory must be based on relatively realistic assumptions about human motivations and rational capacities. Understanding who has vested interests and sufficient clout to block changes in the allocation and distribution of wealth are prerequisites to the design of appropriate institutions of government and law and to the determination of socially desirable policies.

This section surveys what the major political economic theories of the nineteenth and twentieth centuries had to say about human motivations and reason and how they incorporated policy, politics, and power into their analyses of society. Our emphasis is on the approaches that achieved a fairly high level of hegemony among government decision-makers, but we recognize that there were heterodox views and, often, significant opposition to the status quo. We shall highlight some of the most important as we proceed.

---

[8] For an accessible summary as well as a discussion of the research that followed, see Kahneman (2011).

Our review enables us to reconsider past contributions as we develop building blocks for the future. It also enables us to identify missteps caused by problematic assumptions or problematic means for achieving general well-being. The history of political economy prompts us to recognize the role of philosophy, psychology, political science, legal studies, and sociology as well as economics in constructing a new moral political economy.

The Classical Political Economists

> In the eighteenth and nineteenth centuries, the key progenitors of modern liberalism ... did not abandon the good or disregard civic life. They did not glorify personal interests. They were not actors above the fray or outside history.
>
> Kalyvas and Katznelson 2008, 15

Adam Smith provided the most famous early articulation of capitalist political economy in his *Wealth of Nations* (Smith 1986 [1776]). His words in this text have contributed perhaps more than anyone else's to the view of humans as motivated purely by self-interest and of markets as guided by an invisible hand. But they should not be – as they have been – taken out of the context of his full oeuvre or of his times.

Smith lived in a historical period that alerted him to the need for fundamental alteration of the political economy. What drove his theory was the combination of his view of human nature and reason, his recognition of a major transformation in commercial society, and his opposition to mercantilism. Equally important was his belief that the institution of private property was the basis of liberty and an important engine of the market.

Smith was very much a member of the Scottish Enlightenment who thought that passions, such as sympathy and recognition, were the grounding for both morality and cooperation. Indeed, as many now recognize, Smith's *Theory of Moral Sentiments* (1982 [1759]) is foundational for *Wealth of Nations,* as well as for his work on jurisprudence and on rhetoric.[9] For example, Nobel economist Vernon Smith argues, "behavior in *Sentiments* is about conduct, and its propriety or fitness with the rules of fair play .... Hence, *Sentiments* provided the property right foundations that enabled markets to support knowledge specialization and wealth creation ... under third party enforcement rules" (Smith 2012, 3). In this and other readings, Adam Smith stressed rules and norms that contribute to maximizing society's wealth by constraining the behavior of self-interested individuals operating in competitive markets.

---

[9] See, for example, Hirschman (1977); Fleischacker (2004); Kalyvas and Katznelson (2008); Smith (2012); Bowles (2016); Weingast (2017); Smith and Wilson (2019); Liu and Weingast (forthcoming).

But as important to his thinking were the recognition of the extraordinary times in which he lived. As industry revolutionized production and commerce, it altered the number and kinds of commodities being trucked and bartered. Simultaneously, enclosures displaced the agricultural population who fled to the cities and manufacturing hubs, consequently increasing and cheapening the industrial labor pool.

His observations about industrialization led to one of his most important contributions: the specialization and division of labor. Indeed, without that, the invisible hand might not give rise to the wealth of nations. Specialization already existed in an agricultural economy, but it became even more important in an increasingly industrial one. The new technologies that accelerated industrialization, such as steam-powered machines, enhanced human productivity by enabling people to make more with less effort, at least in principle. They also converted production into discrete components, requiring distinctive knowledge, skills, and thus specialization. This transformation of the organization of work turned individual efforts into a collective process.

Adam Smith and his follower David Ricardo rejected earlier versions of political economy that attributed the source of value to land (Mazzucato 2018, 28–31); for them value rested in production and thus labor. Moreover, both argued that rents from land were the result of a monopoly access to ownership. For Smith, such rents were productive only to the extent they were invested in increased productive capacity rather than in wasteful consumption. Ricardo went further, arguing against the prevailing orthodoxy that rents would be competed away. What ensured the endurance of rents was the power of landlords in the capitalist system (Mazzucato 2018, 43).

For Smith and Ricardo, vested interests were a major obstacle to the realization of the wealth of nations. They were particularly antagonist to the economic doctrine of mercantilism, which the merchant class advocated and disproportionately profited from. Government adoption of mercantilism led to the authorization of monopolies (e.g., The East India Company) and protectionist policies to defend national enterprises from competition.

Both Smith and Ricardo became proponents of the laissez-faire or free market ideology that spread throughout Europe in the nineteenth century. Their work was consistent with the prevailing belief in the harmonious relation between private advantage and the public good. From this belief it follows that any government intervention would corrupt natural market processes, and therefore such intervention ought to be minimal.[10] The key to progress and

---

[10] For an account of the philosophical debt of laissez-faire see Keynes (1926, part 1). For a brief account of the history of equating laissez-faire with "uncompromising non-interference," see Handman, Usher, Stocking, Bladen, Mitchell, Jaffee, Hansen, and Goodrich (1931).

prosperity lay in a free market regulated by competition, a competition that government should ensure rather than constrain on behalf of a particular class.

Implicit in their arguments was an analysis of power. They recognized the role of special and protected interests in delimiting the economic potential of the society, and both argued for changes in legislation and government practice promoted by influential actors, particularly aristocratic landlords and rich merchants. But they also recognized that government had some positive roles. Smith delineated the obligations of "the duty of the sovereign" as national defense, administration of justice, and the provision of public works and public institutions that support commercial productivity but that would not be privately provided. Among these he includes education, religious instruction, and infrastructure (Smith 1986 [1776], book V, chapter 1).

But, for the most part, government should get out of the way, particularly when its policies reduced efficient trade and artificially inhibited the distribution of wealth to all who had contributed to its creation. The implication, however, was an activist effort to protect the market and use government to do so; political economists did not steer clear of politics but were engaged participants. Both Smith and Ricardo argued stridently for the abolition of the Corn Laws, a tariff on imported grains as a means of protecting domestic landowners. Their arguments for free trade were grounded in conceptions of what made for more productive work, investments, and allocation of resources. It also came from a strongly held belief that the result of free trade would be "redistribution away from domestic landowners and industrial capitalists in favor of the poor, because it was the latter who benefited from access to cheaper foreign goods, beginning with foodstuffs" (Janeway 2020, 9).

While Smith and Ricardo expressed sympathy for the plight of the poor, neither offered a solution beyond the unfettered competitive market, which they believed would lift all boats. Both were strongly opposed to taxes and other such government instruments for reallocating rents. Ricardo explicitly opposed wage and hours policy (Ricardo 2001 [1817], 96). He advocated the abolition of the poor laws, which he claimed inhibited the advancement of the working class by blocking the market mechanisms that would lead to a rise in their wages over time. He shared with his friend Thomas Malthus (Malthus 1986) a concern about the prospect that population growth would deflate wages, and he argued that the working class had to learn restraint in terms of family size and consumption patterns. The poor laws, as he interpreted them, discouraged such restraint.

Ricardo offered an important extension of Smith's division and specialization of labor with the theory of "comparative advantage" (Ricardo 2001[1817]).[11]

---

[11] Also, see James Mill (1844 [1821]), chapter III, section IV.

Different countries have different natural endowments and productive capacities and differential costs of growing, fabricating, and transporting. A country may have an absolute advantage in mining gold because they have so much of it, but it should grow and sell cotton if it can do so at a lower price and more efficiently than competitors, that is, if it has a comparative advantage in growing cotton. In other words, a country should take opportunity costs into account when determining production and trade activities. It should not produce something domestically that it can get more cheaply through trade and should produce that which it can do more cheaply than others. Ricardo argued that the benefits to be derived from comparative advantage can only occur if trade barriers are reduced. This argument has clear implications for government policy, implying an opposition to – we will use the term anachronistically here – import substitution.

Implicit in Ricardo's argument – and that of almost all who came after him[12] – was the acceptance of "Say's Law" (Say 1834 [1803]), which argues that supply creates its own demand and that, therefore, a production glut of unsold goods is theoretically impossible and only, at worst, a temporary problem. Thus, ceteris paribus, the economy will operate at full capacity with income and employment rising as production does. This assumed away all of the issues we now consider the domain of macroeconomics.

While Ricardo, therefore, shared with Smith the presumption that a free market regulated by competition would lead to progress, his was a far more pessimistic conclusion than Smith's. His analysis led him to infer that landlord power would persist, resulting in increased misery for agricultural and industrial workers, given that the price of commodities would continue to be kept artificially high while wages remained too low to purchase all that was required for a reasonable subsistence. Population growth would only make the situation worse.

It is the combination of Malthus's and Ricardo's theories that, many claim, perhaps apocryphally (Thompson 2013), gave economics the name of the "dismal science." Certainly, the two of them offered insights into how the economy can be structured poorly and thus perform poorly, if there are not policies and practices – governmental or, as they preferred, at the individual level – that change the population dynamics or inhibit non-productive rent-seeking.

The debate over the appropriate form and role of government and who should be represented in it continued as a theme for the classical political economists

---

[12] Notable exceptions were Marx and, later, Keynes, who upended Say's Law in his *General Theory* (Keynes 1936).

who followed, most notably John Stuart Mill (1882). All based their ideas on articulated and relatively realistic conceptions of human motivation and behavior as well as ideas about what kind of governmental laws and arrangements might encourage – or discourage – people to act in ways that would produce a collective benefit to the society. Their arguments generally incorporated politics in the form of the passage of legislation although they disagreed among them about the best policies. Significantly, all included an analysis of which special interests held inordinate power that could block the achievement of the common good.

Alternative Visions

The classical political economists argued among themselves, sometimes quite stridently, but they all shared a commitment to capitalism and to the free market. There were other theorists and activists, however, who opposed either the economic system altogether or the practices and policies that were by-products of capitalism and its justificatory frameworks. Most notable were anarchists, labor movements, and socialists.

Antagonism to capitalist excesses preceded the theories of Smith and evolved throughout the nineteenth century. Eighteenth-century movements in Britain included early communitarian anarchists such as the True Levellers and the Diggers. Led and inspired by Protestant religious reformer Gerrard Winstanley, they appropriated enclosed common land to cultivate with all those who share the work and then its products. Winstanley argued enclosure violated the social contract between the common people and parliament, which owed them a debt for their service in the recent struggle with Cromwell's Model Army (Corns, Hughes, and Loewenstein 2009, 12–13).

By the end of the century, the anarchist approach received philosophical grounding with the publication of William Godwin's *An Enquiry Concerning Political Justice* (Godwin 1793). Inspired by such American radicals as Thomas Paine as well as by utilitarianism, he continued to update his arguments. The third and final edition in 1798 reflected the influence of his recently deceased wife, the famous early feminist philosopher and activist, Mary Wollstonecraft (Philp 2017).

The industrial transformation of work in the early nineteenth century spawned embryonic versions of the labor movement. The Luddites, famous for breaking machinery in resistance to industrialization, were followed by a long history of efforts by working people to collectively organize to demand better working conditions, wages, and voice, both at work and in politics.

American political economist Henry George's late-nineteenth-century arguments (George, Peddle, and Peirce 2016) were extremely popular, and they influenced Progressive Era thinking and policy proposals. An American political progressive, he advocated the secret ballot, women's suffrage, the abolition of debtors' prisons, an expansion of publicly provided services and protections, and changes in numerous laws that protected monopolies and that harmed the worker and the poor. He believed in free trade but was anti-monopoly. His most famous proposition was the "single tax" on the economic rents and unimproved value of land, which he deemed common property. His argument that the tax on land would be sufficient to support public goods became known as the Henry George Theorem. It continues to be under discussion as a serious proposal (Arnott and Stiglitz 1979; Posner and Weyl 2018).

But the most important and influential of those offering an alternative approach was undoubtedly Karl Marx.

The Marxian Critique of Classical Political Economy

By the 1840s, when Karl Marx began writing, the industrial revolution further shifted the relative economic power of landowners, merchants, and industrialists. Marx had a different perspective on power than Smith or Ricardo. He took the labor theory of value to its logical conclusion, leading him to advocate for structural change that went far beyond legislative reform. The power relationships themselves required fundamental transformation. First, government is always the captive of the ruling elite (Marx and Engels 1978 [1848]). Second, the so-called free market is designed to reward those with property rights over the means of production rather than create genuine free exchange. In contradistinction to Ricardo, for Marx it was not government programs or landowners or lack of personal restraint that prevented workers from becoming more prosperous; it was the power of the capitalists. Yes, workers are in contractual relations that give them pay in return for labor, but they become what he dubbed "wage slaves" who have little choice but to accept what they are offered in terms of salary, hours, and working conditions (Marx 1974 [1867], chapter VI, 254–5).

> He, who before was the money owner, now strides in front as capitalist; the possessor of labor-power follows as his laborer. The one with an air of importance, smirking, intent on business; the other, timid and holding back, like one who is bringing his own hide to market and has nothing to expect but – a hiding. (Marx 1974 [1867])

For Marx, the labor market was dehumanizing, but so, too, were the work and working conditions. The factory might have ensured a division and specialization of labor, but it also created a new setting for both hierarchy and unequal power. Owners, through their managers and machines, controlled the pace and hours of work.[13] His analysis of the working day (Marx 1974 [1867], chapter X) is an in-depth sociological treatise of the servitude of workers and the indifference of bosses to workers' need for breaks, adequate sleeping time, education, and recreation. It is also a sophisticated political account of the incentives for progressive legislation, passed by a parliament dominated by capitalist interests. The productivity of workers depended on better treatment, but no single proprietor could impose shorter working hours without losing the competitive edge. This is a collective-action problem, which only government could solve by acting in the interests of the capitalists it served and thus enforcing on all the standard each privately desired. It is important to note that the legislation was not a response to worker power. By the mid-nineteenth century, workers in England were beginning to gain some political influence through mobilization, but their influence was limited by the restrictions on unionization and the franchise. The situation was equally problematic and possibly worse for US workers well into the twentieth century.

Like Ricardo, Marx had a dynamic theory of change. The political economy would transform over time, but the source of dynamic change was technology, rather than population or demography. Marx's was a more optimistic scenario (at least for those desiring fundamental change in power relationships and equality) than Ricardo's, although only over the *longue durée*. Technological change would lead to a reduced demand for workers and thus a reduced price for their work. The result would be two-staged: first, increased misery experienced by those in the unemployed reserve army of labor; and, second, the decline in the need for private owners and managers of industry, that is, for capitalists. The combination of the two would lead to a revolution led by workers and a consequent revolutionary transformation in the ownership of the means of production and a new post-capitalist political economy.

Marx's model was as flawed as Ricardo's. Both relied on problematic assumptions. For Ricardo, it was the belief that landowner power would continue unabated; he did not predict the power industrial capitalists would achieve. For Marx, it was the assumption that workers would combine to overthrow the system. But the working class did not – for the most part – become revolutionary in their mobilization or their votes (Przeworski and Sprague 1986). Marx also did not anticipate the development of a significant

---

[13] It was not until Ronald Coase (1937) that contemporary and standard economics even began to bring power relationships within the firm into their models. Of course, some institutional economists, some labor economists, and "radical" economists had recognized this, but, with the exception of Veblen (1953 [1912], 1914), few theorized the problem until the 1970s (see, e.g., Marglin 1974, 1975; Edwards, Reich, and Weisskopf 1978; Edwards 1979).

middle class with interests and influence of its own. Nor did he recognize that government, which he had dismissed as a tool of the ruling class, had autonomous power and capacities. With the extension of the franchise and the rise of serious electoral politics, some governments were willing to introduce policies regulating working conditions, pay, social insurance, and even policies that went further in abrogating the privileges and wealth of the capitalists.

Severing the Links with Politics and Society

The marginalist revolution ended the efforts to incorporate into political economic frameworks realistic assumptions about human motivation and rationality, the values needed to support a vision of a good society, and analyses of politics and power.

The marginalists assumed that individual actors, generally consumers, have fixed subjective preferences that inform their choices in a world of scarcity. Consumers purchase, based on the relative marginal utility, what each additional increment adds to satisfying one's wants. Marginal utility decreases as consumption needs are satisfied and increases as a desired good becomes harder to obtain. Conversely, decisions about production depend on the marginal costs of producing the goods being sought. Supply and demand, therefore, determine the equilibrium price, which equates the marginal utility to the purchaser and the marginal cost to the producer of the last item bought or offered. Working at a time of unprecedented scientific progress, the marginalists (most notably, William Stanley Jevons, Alfred Marshall, and Leon Walras)[14] shrouded economics in the rigors of mathematics. Their work derived from physics as it was understood in the late nineteenth century, with its insistence on fundamental laws deduced and tested mathematically,[15] and differential calculus gave them the capacity to evaluate marginal changes in variables.

With the rise of the marginalist revolution came both the decoupling of economics from society and the extreme simplification of assumptions about human decision-making. The result was increased precision in the models and, presumably, greater predictive capacity, achieved by obliterating the richness and complexity of human action and institutions. The world of the marginalists was largely institution- and context-free: the actual rules of the game and norms

---

[14] Economic historian David Chilosi pointed out to us that there were differences among the marginalists in regard to the relationship between theory and reality. For Jevons, math described reality (Jevons 1965 [1888]). Marshall perceived a tradeoff between tractability and realistic assumptions (Marshall 1936 [1920]). Walras believed science was based on abstraction and thus was not concerned with realism (Walras 2013 [1889]).

[15] For recent elaborations of the history of economics and the role of the marginalists, see Beinhocker (2006) and Mazzucato (2018).

of a society hardly mattered. This world was also frictionless: there were almost no transaction costs, and individual choices led to aggregate outcomes free of persuasion, influence, or coercion. Power and powerful interests had no place in the marginalist model.

The marginalists shared with classical economists the understanding of the world as one of scarcity: the allocation of scarce resources was one of the primary roles played by the market. However, the claim was both mathematically and philosophically underdeveloped without a yardstick by which to gauge the efficacy and efficiency of markets. The utilitarian argument of providing the greatest good for the greatest number had been the welfare standard, but it was difficult to measure and thus to apply. With the wrong kind of application, it also could lead to undesirable impediments to innovation in technology and organizational structure.

By the turn of the twentieth century, the search for a better standard culminated in the concept of welfare maximization. Vilfredo Pareto (2013 [1906]) is most often identified with this move, particularly through his idea of Pareto-optimal equilibrium, that is, the point at which no one is better off at the expense of someone becoming worse off. Pareto optimality presumes fairness in the allocation of resources since capital and labor, the two factors of production, each receive their marginal product. Over time, it proved an important guide to policy and practice.

Economists still advanced the mantra of free markets. Yet, in the late nineteenth century, as business concentrated and arguably upended the free market, the marginalists were more fearful of "ruinous competition" and "overproduction" than of monopoly. They became either outright indifferent to or opposed anti-trust legislation (Hovenkamp 2009), which they considered futile, given the growing belief that business monopolies tend to be natural and inevitable (Letwin 1981, 71–7).[16] Unlike their classical predecessors, they lacked a clear vision of the good society; they were uninterested in analyzing when and if a particular set of special interests had structural power. Power relations were outside the scope of their analyses. The abstract conception of the rational agent, optimizing utility under conditions of certainty about the future consequences of today's decision, led ultimately to the practice of applying a simplified, noncontextual model to choices made across all human domains of action.

The marginalist approach has remained the dominant influence on economics until now, although, as we shall see, it has taken various paths, some of them quite transformative of the original models.

---

[16] The legal profession, more than the economics profession, provided policy guidance at that point in history for one of the most pressing economic issues of the day (Thelen forthcoming).

Alternative Visions

The most important early-twentieth-century critic of the marginalist approach was Thorstein Veblen, considered by some (Robinson 1979; Camic and Hodgson 2011, 37) as the most original and greatest economist of his era. Like his classical predecessors, his analysis was alert to social forces and to history and based on a model of human reason and motivation informed by the latest advances in psychology. He is best known for his idea of a leisure class (Veblen 1953 [1912]) and his early recognition of the force of consumerism. His famous phrase, "invention is the mother of necessity" (Veblen 1914, 316), articulates how the availability of products shapes tastes and preferences, making people want and believe they need items that may be neither essential nor healthy. However, from our perspective, his most important contributions were those he made to institutional evolutionary economics.

Veblen drew on, and contributed to, both pragmatic philosophy and instinct psychology, emphasizing the importance of habit and instinct in human behavior. The psychological underpinnings of his arguments led him to object to the marginalists' simplified version of human decision-making, which he famously described in an 1898 essay:

> The hedonistic conception of man is that of a lightning calculator of pleasures and pains, who oscillates like a homogeneous globule of desire of happiness under the impulse of stimuli that shift him about the area, but leave him intact. He has neither antecedent nor consequent. He is an isolated, definitive human datum, in stable equilibrium except for the buffets of the impinging forces that displace him in one direction or another. (Veblen 1898, 389)

This passage indicates not only Veblen's critique of marginalist psychology but also of its static model.

An early institutionalist and a precursor of today's evolutionary economics, he argued that individuals created institutions as embodiments of culture and norms of conduct, which then influenced future individuals. For Veblen, institutions had a conservative tendency, inhibiting certain behaviors and change, but also a transformative possibility as changes in society, including technology, altered instincts and led to demands for different arrangements. Individuals, although molded by society and its institutions, were prime movers for change and for institutional adaptation. Throughout his career, Veblen sought a theory of endogenous evolution of economic and social institutions.

Veblen's critique failed to become the orthodoxy. His arguments did not provide ammunition to the powers that be, or to those whom economic changes might empower. While he certainly had colleagues and followers, he did not gain a popular audience or create reasons for popular mobilization. Veblen "was insufficiently engaged with the analysis of practical alternatives to leave us with much of value in this area. He was a dissenting rather than a practical radical" (Camic and Hodgson 2011, 36). However, like that of Henry George, Veblen's work resonates with contemporary concerns and is receiving renewed interest.

What did come to dominate the second half of the twentieth century were two competing responses to the world wars and the multiple recessions and depressions of the first half of the twentieth century. Both Keynsianism and the new classical economists relied on mathematics and tools of marginalist economics but to very different effects.

Keynesianism

> He heard them crying the news in the street. And shrugging his shoulders applied himself to the great green board on which were pinned sheets of symbols: a frolic of xs controlled by ys and embraced by more cryptic symbols still: which, if juggled together would eventually, he was sure, positive, produce the one word, the simple, the sufficient the comprehensive word which will solve all problems forever. It was time to begin. He began.
>
> Virginia Woolf on her great friend John Maynard Keynes (quoted in Carter 2020, 17–18)

If there was one word, it was demand, but that would be a poor summary of the contributions of John Maynard Keynes. Yes, he advanced a political economy that encouraged consumer demand by giving a strong role to government intervention through fiscal instruments and public works. Equally importantly, he recognized and incorporated the significance of uncertainty, which he distinguished from risk; the second could be calculated, the first not. Thus, rational calculations could, at best, reveal what the alternatives might be, given different scenarios, but could not determine which scenario would actually exist.

For Keynes, calculations are not always at the heart of the choices people make. In his view, actions often are reflections of "animal spirits … a spontaneous urge to action rather than inaction, and not as the outcome of a weighted average of quantitative benefits multiplied by quantitative probabilities" (Keynes 1936, 161).[17] Indeed, his books are marked by a rich psychology in which emotions, illusions, and "animal spirits" could undercut rational decision-making. His approach to human motivations also emphasized the role of government in preventing panic in the population, leading to runs on the banks or inappropriately protective saving behavior. Government has an important role in maintaining and, if need be, restoring public confidence by demonstrating competence and providing credible assurances of policies that would make things

---

[17] This became an important concept for the behavioral economists. See, e.g., Akerlof and Schiller (2010).

better. Evoking confidence and optimism in the population are key to keeping the system afloat.

A student of Alfred Marshall, Keynes was a highly skilled mathematical economist, but his approach was more akin to that of the classical political economists than to the marginalists. According to his most recent biographer, "Keynes was a philosopher of war and peace, the last of the Enlightenment intellectuals who pursued political theory, economics, and ethics as a unified design." (Carter 2020, 13) He understood his work as contributing to economics, yes, but also to ethics, which meant to him ensuring a good life for as many as possible and, in the process, preserving civilization from the threats that surrounded it (Mann 2017).

Where Keynes sharply distinguished himself from the classical political economists was in his break with laissez-faire. He did not believe markets were able to self-regulate, and he repudiated Say's Law that supply created its own demand. Keynes articulated his alternative most clearly in *The General Theory* (1936) where he argued that, in fact, supply could outrun demand, that incomes and employment could fall significantly and disastrously, and that the system could not move to a better equilibrium without significant government intervention. His was an economy in which financial interests dominated, money was an asset and not merely a means of exchange or unit of account, and decisions about saving and investment influenced other sectors of the economy, notably production and trade. The fact that these decisions were made under conditions of uncertainty made it more likely that there would be unintended, unexpected, and disastrous consequences.

The Great Depression provided fuel for his arguments. From his perspective, the Depression demonstrated how economies could be stuck in a bad equilibrium of deep unemployment, something current (and past) economic dogma could neither predict nor explain. The only way out was for government to spend in order to create the aggregate demand that would ultimately lead to a new and better equilibrium. This did not, however, make him a proponent of unbounded government: "The important thing for Government is not to do things which individuals are doing already, and do them a little better or a little worse; but to do those things which at present are not done at all" (Keynes 1926, 317). But he proposed government action for more than the occasional correction of market failures or free rider problems or even for the particular harms caused by the Great Depression. Examples of where government action was required included increased state management of the labor market and of the monetary, currency, and credit systems as well as the development of public works.

By the account of others and in his own view, Keynes adopted a Middle Way (Skidelsky 1994, 437); he was neither a socialist advocating central planning nor an unfettered capitalist who felt the state should never intervene. Rather he wanted government to step in and regulate private industry and finance where it could not regulate itself. "What Marx had diagnosed as a distributional struggle to be settled by power, Keynes saw as a problem of insufficient demand to be remedied by expertise" (Skidelsky 1994, 439, 569–70).

Like his classical predecessors, Keynes identified economic interests whose political power often thwarted good public policy. For Smith, it was the merchants, for Ricardo the landed aristocracy, for Marx the capitalist owners of industry, and for Veblen the leisure class. From the time of the economic slump in Britain following World War I until his death in 1946, Keynes regularly railed against the shortsighted practices of bankers and stockbrokers, that is, financial capital. He took his vision and ideas into the public arena, where he transformed policies and decisions during at least two major economic crises and two world wars. He appealed to and allied with prime ministers, presidents, and other political leaders to help him turn his ideas into practical policies. And he worked to institutionalize those ideas and practices, as exemplified by the 1944 Bretton Woods agreement, which created a new international monetary arrangement with fixed exchange and moved the world away from the gold standard.

The legacy of Keynes is a complex one. Some of those who claimed to follow in his footsteps, perhaps most notably John Hicks and Paul Samuelson, further mathematized Keynes's contributions. Keynes himself expressed concerns about this move (Keynes 1937). Keynes's colleague Joan Robinson labeled the approach of some American Keynesians, among them Paul Samuelson and Robert Solow, "bastard Keynesianism" (Skidelsky 1994, 538, 621). Their offense was less their mathematics than their evocation of macroeconomic full employment policies while actually advancing microeconomic models aimed at more limited efficiency gains.

Before Keynes, there was nothing labeled macroeconomics, but after him it was a central part of economics. He recognized that crises were recurrent – after all he lived through several major slumps and wars – and that the system did not always self-correct, that is, return to equilibrium. Most importantly, from our perspective, he combined a rich psychology with an equally rich philosophically based vision of a better world best achieved through a deeper understanding of economics and the recognition of an important role for government. Thus, it is hardly surprising that, since the Global Financial Crisis, there is a new obsession with Keynes.

Alternative Visions

There were several alternative visions to the one advocated by Keynes. Friedrich Hayek's will be discussed at length below, given his pivotal role in the creation of the new classical economics. The 1930s and 1940s were also a period when two eminent practitioners of institutional evolutionary economics, John Commons (1924, 1934) and Joseph Schumpeter (1942), produced their most important work.

Commons and Schumpeter shared with Veblen a perspective that was skeptical of the market as self-regulating, and they both integrated sociological and political with economic factors in their analyses of the economy (Papageorgiou, Katselidis, and Michaelides 2013). For Commons, this led to a recognition of the important role of collective action in bringing about change and a deep interest in labor as actors and focus of policy. But it was Schumpeter who more forcefully foreshadowed many of the central questions in contemporary political economy.

A fan of capitalism, Schumpeter nonetheless predicted its demise due to problems within the system itself. The principal problems were the undermining of the entrepreneur and the expansion of the role of government due to democratic pressures.

The entrepreneur was central to processes of "creative destruction," the concept for which Schumpeter is perhaps best known.[18] Creative destruction was the engine of capitalism, which, subject to technological and organizational changes, "incessantly revolutionizes the economic structure from within, incessantly destroying the old one, incessantly creating a new one" (Schumpeter 1942, 83). Technological and entrepreneurial innovation were the sources of economic growth but also the catalysts to business cycles generated by the waxing and waning of investment. Schumpeter argued that the institutionalization of entrepreneurial innovations made the entrepreneur secondary to managers and shareholders. The consequence would be the decline of capitalism.

Schumpeter was concerned about another source of power that could undermine capitalism beside managerial big business: the power of the people. Although he shared with Keynes a view that capitalism went through waves that were not always self-correcting, Schumpeter's corrective was not the expansion of government but the empowerment of entrepreneurial leadership in both the economy and government. His fear of popular democracy was influenced by his observations of both fascism and socialism but also of how easily even democratic citizens are manipulated.

---

[18] Schumpeter's "creative destruction" bears a kinship with the contemporary idea of disruption.

Schumpeter's analysis of the problems of democracy and his partial solution turned out to have a direct influence on political science. He argued for a minimal role for voters and therefore a minimalist definition of democracy: free competition by potential leaders for free votes. This conception remains central in the debate about the appropriate definition of democracy (Przeworski 1999; Mackie 2009), and it proved a precursor to rational and social choice accounts of elections (Mitchell 1984).

Far more heterodox than Schumpeter was Karl Polanyi.[19] *The Great Transformation* (Polanyi 1957), originally published in 1944, is a critique of market fundamentalism, the belief that markets are self-regulating and thus laissez-faire is the best governmental response. He challenged "quasi-religious certainty expressed by contemporary advocates of market self-regulation" and their reliance on "a claim to truth independent of the kind of empirical investigation that is expected in the social sciences" (Block and Somers 2014, 3). For Polanyi, the economy, one of many human-created institutions, is embedded in the social practices, norms, and governance arrangements of the society. Moreover, it is a myth that the market can be or ever has been self-regulating. It is, in fact, a creation of politics and policy, and it depends on government for its very existence. Despite what so many economists seem to believe, the market, indeed the economy itself, is neither autonomous nor subject to laws of its own.

Not surprisingly, Polanyi's view of democracy was the opposite of Schumpeter's, Hayek's, and Friedman's. The role of a democratic government and politics is to constrain the worst excesses of the market and to make it work for the betterment of all. For the government to succeed at this task, the citizens must be fully engaged and participatory, a theme we shall return to in Section 3. It is, after all, the well-being and concerns of the populace that are fundamentally at stake. Equally important, it is their pressure, through mobilization and votes, that gives the government the authority it needs to hold economic institutions accountable.

Polanyi's theory of change is encapsulated in his concept of the "double movement." Whenever market fundamentalism gains dominance, governments initiate policies that are ultimately both destabilizing and dehumanizing. The effect is resistance and a countervailing movement of thought and action. We may well be in such a moment now, and Polanyi's recent upsurge in popularity indicates how much he speaks to our current concerns.

---

[19] We draw heavily here from Fred Block and Margaret Somers (Block and Somers 2014).

Neoclassical Economics

Neoclassical economics builds on the marginalist revolution and informs almost all prevailing economic models – and textbooks. The neoclassical model assumes that humans are individualistic, self-interested, rational, utility maximizers with complete information and perfect foresight. They have consistent and stable preferences, do not suffer from biases (or their biases are randomly distributed), are context independent, and have infinite cognitive abilities and resources. Markets exist in a state of equilibrium determined by price, where supply obeys the law of diminishing marginal returns and demand that of diminishing marginal utility. There are zero transaction costs, and time is discrete or irrelevant. Change, or disequilibrium, is a "shock."

Keynes influenced a major strand of post–World War II neoclassical economists, some of whom became the most influential economists of their generation. They accepted the Keynesian emphasis on a constructive role of government in creating financial stability and in expanding government expenditure as a fiscal policy. Internationally, this approach led to Bretton Woods and the Marshall Plan. Domestically, it led to a massive rebuilding of infrastructure and extension of government programs for education, housing, and social insurance.

The contributions of major thinkers, such as Nobel laureates Paul Samuelson (Samuelson 1938, 1998) and Kenneth Arrow and Gerard Debreu (Arrow and Debreu 1954), gave mathematics a prominent role for theory-building and enabled them to produce rigorous formalizations of the functioning of markets. They upheld the ambitions of economics to emulate the physical sciences. But they largely ignored the contributions of the humanities and social sciences that Keynes and Smith and other great political economists felt were essential to understanding human motivation and societies. A concern about societal well-being remained but was measured almost exclusively by aggregate economic growth.

This group of economists were, however, concerned with policy. The Roosevelt administration hired economists by the drove, and in the 1950s and 1960s, some of these economists had become – in the words we use today – influencers. Many were macroeconomists. Many engaged with political actors as advisors or to advance favored policies. But with few exceptions, they did not incorporate accounts of interest groups or conceptions of political power into their economic thinking.[20]

---

[20] One major exception was Arrow (1951), whose social choice account of democratic decision-making (and its limits) has exerted an immense influence on political science.

Nor did they adequately recognize, let alone deal with, some of the continuing structural problems of inequality and poverty afflicting capitalism. The myth persists that the post–World War II years, especially in the United States, were a period of extraordinary growth and prosperity. And, in many ways, they were. The developed democracies, even those devastated by the war, saw a huge growth in infrastructure, physical and social. Highways were built, ports modernized, and education extended at all levels. But the economists of that era seemed largely unaware – at least in their theorizing – of the "other America" (Harrington 1962; see also Galbraith 1969), those impoverished or suffering from the inequities caused by race and gender discrimination. The Korean War marked the beginning of the continuing era of "small" wars. And it was a period in which the paranoia, intolerance, and partisanship of McCarthyism put democracy itself in peril.

Keynesianism dominated the post–World War II era, but it was far from homogenous. Two of Keynes's most famous followers dissented from the neoclassical variant. Joan Robinson offered an account of Keynesianism meant to address the evolution of capitalism over the long term (Robinson 1969).[21] John Kenneth Galbraith-an institutional economist who had considerable influence within the Democratic Party and played several key roles, particularly in the John F. Kennedy administration-was one of the few economists of his day who took power seriously and analyzed the role of government as an important source of countervailing power to that of big business (Galbraith 1952). By the 1970s, he was emphasizing a problem that continues to plague contemporary political economists: neither competition nor government was keeping the major corporations in check (Galbraith 1971).

However, these alternatives to the orthodoxy were not the impetus for the demise of Keynesianism as the dominant paradigm. Stagflation was the reason it lost its preeminence. The prevailing economists had not predicted nor prepared for the combination of inflation and high unemployment that reduced economic output and made the economy stagnant. Just as the unpredicted levels of high unemployment gave Keynesianism its opening in the 1930s, stagflation made it possible for the new classical and supply side economists to grab the center stage.

The New Classical Economists

Keynes's *General Theory* (Keynes 1936) was a major provocation to the Austrian and Chicago School economists, who were market fundamentalists

---

[21] Other Marxists, most notably Paul Baran and Paul Sweezy, argued that Keynesian solutions would delay but not inhibit inevitable stagflation (Baran and Sweezy 1966).

eager to constrain government interventions in the economy. First in the United Kingdom and in the United States, and then throughout much of the capitalist world, they overturned the Keynesian framework of political economy as a guide to government policy.

Frank Knight, the celebrated Chicago economist, helped recruit Friedrich Hayek, the influential Austrian economist, to Chicago.[22] They shared a commitment to the free market as the best way to protect liberty (Skidelsky 1994, 577). Indeed, this view was shared by the many others who joined the Mont Pelerin Society, which Hayek founded to combat a paradigm they believed to be both wrong economically and problematic in its aspirations (Burgin 2012). They were committed to the jointly entwined (for them) goals of democracy and economic growth. They were not against all government, but felt the primary role of regulation and intervention was to remove restraints on the market and ensure the forms of competition that they believed helped make markets so effective.

Their arguments and models gave support to a growing movement to reduce the role of government in the economy and society, to lower taxes, and to promote a market ideology even in countries – such as Chile in the 1970s and 1980s – that were notoriously repressive. By making government smaller and poorer, the aim was to reduce dependence on government as opposed to the private sector, and to loosen the constraints on markets, firms, financial institutions, and individuals. The same measures also reduced confidence in government, largely because of its diminished capacity to deliver.

The contributions of the new classicals should not be lost in the flood of criticism directed upon them as their era of dominance draws to a close. Hayek, for example, articulated the importance of tacit knowledge, knowledge that is generally local and difficult to articulate (Oguz 2010). Markets, he argued, were far more capable than government at capturing and using such tacit knowledge. He shared with Keynes an emphasis on the importance of uncertainty facing decision-makers although they emphasized different actors: Keynes focused on consumers, brokers, bankers, and other market participants; Hayek was more concerned about policymakers.

Another well-known leader of Mont Pelerin, Nobel laureate Milton Friedman, not only brought into the mainstream a new monetary theory (Friedman 1968), he also derived from his economic models arguments for a negative income tax, school vouchers, and regulations to limit forms of monopoly that might interfere with the market, most notably monopolies over

---

[22] Knight, it should be noted, emphasized the distinction between risk and uncertainty even before Keynes. And, as earlier mentioned, Hayek emphasized uncertainty.

labor such as unions and the American Medical Association (Friedman and Friedman 1980). Gary Becker and George Stigler, also Nobel Prize winners, interrogated the theory of preference and allowed for a plurality of choices (Stigler and Becker 1977). Becker's (1964) work on human capital was ground-breaking in recognizing that workers embody a stock of knowledge, skills, creativity, and other resources that are affected by investments and vary in value.

⨎   At the same time, these were also the economists who most embodied the imperialism of the discipline. Becker felt comfortable applying a decontextualized, abstract model of decision-making to virtually every sphere of human activity, including discrimination, marriage, and crime and punishment (Becker 1957, 1968, 1974). Similarly, James Buchanan and Gordon Tullock applied economics to political decision-making (Buchanan and Tullock 1965). They offered a model of politics as a series of voluntary exchanges for mutual advantage, clarifying the problems both resolved and created by mechanisms such as logrolling. They did not actually ignore political power; rather, like Schumpeter, they distrusted popular power and suggested means to contain it. In particular, they argued against majority rule and for procedures based on unanimity. Buchanan continued to write on these issues, particularly emphasizing constitutional or fundamental rules that were long-lasting and that determined the procedures of legislatures and other governmental bodies (Buchanan 1999).

The new classicals were extremely influential on the mindsets of the public, public officials, and academics. The *Reader's Digest* translation and abridgment of Hayek's *The Road to Serfdom* made Hayek one of the most widely read popular authors of his time (Burgin 2012, 87–93). Friedman's two popular texts (Friedman and Friedman 1962; Friedman and Friedman 1980), coauthored with his wife, Rose Friedman, were bestsellers and the basis for a TV series he hosted. The new classicals founded new disciplines and subdisciplines. For example, Buchanan and Tullock were a major force behind the Public Choice Society, and Ronald Coase was influential in creating. These new approaches shaped the training of government policymakers, staff, and justices (Teles 2008).[23]

Alternative Visions

Even in its heyday, there were challenges to the new classical approach. One of them came from those who founded the Union for Radical Political Economics

---

[23] MacLean (2017) argues that Buchanan's work stoked the radical right, but this is a controversial claim (Burns 2018).

(URPE) in 1968. Some of the most important critiques of contemporary capitalism and economics came from their ranks. For example, they helped identify the segmented labor force (Edwards, Gordon, and Reich 1982). The white, unionized, largely male workers had – at that time at least – decent jobs and benefits and enjoyed real intergenerational opportunities for economic and social improvement. In contrast, people of color and women generally had dead-end and poorly paid jobs. The segmentation was reinforced by an educational system that provided differential skills and training based on class, race, and gender (Bowles and Gintis 1977). Their analyses built on an understanding of class power and of vested interests well served by the status quo. The goal of the URPE economists was to analyze the base and consequences of such power but also to change it.

Other challenges came from a group of eminent economists, among them Nobel laureates Joseph Stiglitz, Edmund Phelps, Paul Krugman, and Paul Romer. Stiglitz won the prize for his work on asymmetric information, Phelps for his analyses of intertemporal tradeoffs in macroeconomic theory, Krugman for innovations in trade theory, and Romer for endogenous growth theory. They used their standing to launch critiques of the failures of the prescriptions of unregulated markets and free trade. They and others were eager to promote theory and policies to enable greater well-being among a much larger segment of the population. While building on neoclassical economics, they recognized the important role of government and the need for active intervention in the economy to ensure a greater inclusiveness and more equitable distribution of resources among both people and countries.

There were also challenges to the assumptions embodied in most economic modeling: these came, principally, from behavioral economics and complexity theory. Behavioral economics (Thaler 1991; Camerer, Loewenstein, and Rabin 2004; Thaler and Sunstein 2008) draws on psychological insights about decision-making to create better and more realistic models of choice. While hardly undoing either the new classical or neoclassical economic model of human behavior, these insights portray a more complex, fallible, and social human. Intended to contribute to the capacity of governments to encourage citizens to take advantage of policies, behavioral economics models also have implications for the ways technology companies and politically motivated media can influence how people behave (Ward 2020).

Institutionalized in the founding of the Santa Fe Institute (SFI) in 1984, complexity theory was originally an interdisciplinary endeavor that brought together natural and physical scientists, social scientists, and even novelists. Economic complexity theorists reject the assumptions of standard economics, particularly the idea of rational agents and stable equilibria. They perceive "the economy as a system not necessarily in equilibrium, but rather as one where agents constantly change their actions and strategies in response to the outcomes they mutually create" (Arthur, Beinhocker, and Stanger 2020, location 147). One of its earliest proponents and SFI's first resident fellow was W. Brian Arthur, who recognized that increasing returns as well as diminishing returns are present in economies and can lead to lock-in (Arthur 1989). An interesting example is the QWERTY typewriter (David 1985).

Bringing Politics Back into Political Economy

> Even though modern economies are quite different from the economy so flatteringly depicted by the classical economists and so bitterly by Dickens and Marx, it is a fact ... that economic life in the real world today constitutes a *political* economy ... In this book the authors have sought to incorporate certain aspects of politics and economics into a single consistent body of theory.
>
> Dahl and Lindblom 1965 [1953], preface, xxi

As Robert Dahl and Charles Lindblom remind us, politics and power matter in political economy. But despite their best efforts in the 1950s, and those of many scholars who followed them, most economists continued, indeed still continue, to ignore the contributions of political science. Political scientists, however, forged ahead in incorporating the theoretical and methodological advances of economists. This led to the development of new approaches such as social choice and rational choice. It also led, by the early 1980s, to a political economy that combines a sophisticated understanding of human motivation and reason, a vision for a good society, solid economics, and a grasp of power.

Let us begin with rational and social choice. One of the major aims of this new approach was to appropriate the rigor of mathematical economics while also demystifying it in a form that would make political economy an empirical science subject to hypothesis testing with evidence and data. It was not enough to develop a beautiful and logically consistent model; what is derived from the model must be demonstrably true or at least plausible, as measured against actual facts according to the best methods of data collection of the day.

William Riker helped give rational choice theory legitimacy in political science.[24] Not only did he build the "Rochester School" (Amadae and Mesquita 1999), but he also took on questions central to the politics of political economy, such as how minority political coalitions can manipulate legislatures, and how federalism delimits policy agendas and possibly democracy (Riker

---

[24] Of course, there were economists, most notably Arrow (1951), Downs (1957), Buchanan and Tullock (1965), Olson (1965), and Stigler (1971) who were applying economic choice theory to political problems.

1962, 1964). He brought a new rigor to the study of politics, especially American politics.

Riker was part of a larger movement and inspired an army of students and collaborators. The result was a transformation of the study of legislative decision-making, electoral behavior and voting, leadership, federalism, bureaucratic decision-making, and many other key subjects. But these significant advances were not without detractors (Green and Shapiro 1994), who mounted the same objections to the formal theorizing of rational choice that were aimed at similar modeling by economists. In particular, they argued that the theories and their implications were not subject to sufficient empirical testing, and that many of the findings were relatively trivial.

With the development of comparative political economy in the early 1980s,[25] political science began to analyze the central questions of distribution and equity across countries and time. Its practitioners used but transformed the rational choice approach by treating the economy and markets as an institution embedded in other social and political institutions. Robert Bates (1981, 1983), Adam Przeworski (Przeworski and Wallerstein 1982; Przeworski 1985; Przeworski and Sprague 1986; Przeworski and Wallerstein 1988), and Margaret Levi (1981, 1988) attempted to apply economic theories and tools, most notably game theory, to major political questions, such as economic and political development across time and place. Their variant of political economy gave equal status to economic and political actions, actors, and interests as they considered variations in economic growth, productivity, and innovation. These accounts also incorporated context in the form of the institutional arrangements and forms of influence available to different actors in different settings. Most importantly, they put distributional questions and equity considerations at the heart of their investigations.

All of these authors were in locations where they were directly interacting with cutting-edge economists, and some of those economists, most notably Nobel laureate Douglass North, began to engage seriously with political scientists. An economic historian, deeply concerned with the sources of long-term secular change, North began to question some of the assumptions that grounded neoclassical economics. His groundbreaking explorations of institutions and institutional change (North 1981; North and Weingast 1989; North 1990; North,

---

[25] Dahl did engage in a project with Stein Rokkan and others at the Center for Advanced Study in the Behavioral Sciences (CASBS) in the 1950s to make comparative politics truly comparative by engaging in cross-country comparisons rather than single country studies. However, their concern, and that of others who engaged in statistically based research, was more with description and analytics than with political economy per se.

Wallis, and Weingast 2009) incorporated insights from political science about bargaining, sources of influence, ideology, collective action, and the role of law.

North's influence helped shape the new economic institutionalism, the political science variant of the new institutional economics. The Achilles heel of this approach, however, was its inability to fully incorporate an understanding of power (Moe 2005). There was certainly sensitivity to the role of vested interests, conflict, and bargaining resources, but what was usually lacking was recognition that institutions are not simply structures of Pareto-optimal voluntary cooperation in which everyone ends up better off. Rather, institutions are often designed to serve particular interests over others, ensuring that some win while others lose. There was also insufficient concern with the normative goals of society,[26] as well as with human motivations beyond economic interest.[27]

The ideas developed by new economic institutionalists often had direct implications for policy, and some of their practitioners actively engaged with governments and other organizations trying to reform societies. North himself, after he won the Nobel, was constantly asked, as he put it, "to play God to developing countries," advising them on how to develop. His answer, however, was that it took a lot of time for the beliefs and ideas formed in one cultural and structural context to adapt to, and gain acceptance in a new context. Elinor Ostrom (2010b, 2010c), a political scientist who became a Nobel laureate in economics, was more directly interested in policy, particularly policies to ensure the maintenance of common pool resources.

The emergence of historical institutionalism arose independently but also served as an important counterpoint to the new economic institutionalism (Evans, Rueschemeyer, and Skocpol 1985; Thelen and Steinmo 1992; Thelen 1999). Whereas the new economic institutionalism tended to emphasize preferences as given, the historical institutionalists focused on how institutions shape preferences, interests, and choices. Historical institutionalists also emphasized path dependence, including inherited structures of power, as a factor shaping any given institutional configuration. This was distinct from the economist's conception of equilibrium, which happened independently of human intervention. Path dependence, as conceived by political scientists, was an effect not only of history but also of contingency; it was the result of political contestation (Collier and Collier 1991; Pierson 2004).

---

[26] Exceptions include Przeworski (1985) and Roemer (1982, 1988).

[27] Levi (1997) was a partial exception to this in her consideration of ethical commitments. In economics, Bowles (2016) has significantly advanced the integration of moral considerations into economic models.

Initially, this approach was primarily directed toward explaining the past. However, the development of a body of work on "varieties of capitalism" (Hall and Soskice 2001) opened the scope of the analysis to understanding the relationship between structural constraints and viable policy actions. The distinction between liberal and coordinated market economies stressed how the former reduced the role of government and was more negative toward unions, while the latter allowed for more active governments and a greater role for unions. The evolving literature has huge implications for both understanding and also designing industrial relations, vocational training and education, and corporate governance, among other things.[28]

Ultimately, the historical and the new economic institutionalists began interacting, integrating each other's insights. The result is a large body of work that emphasizes the emergence and impact of voters, particularly middle-class voters, and the evolution of parties to account for the variation in democratic political economies (e.g., Boix 1998; Acemoglu and Robinson 2006; Kitschelt and Wilkinson 2007; Scheve and Stasavage 2009; Ansell and Samuels 2014; Díaz Cayeros, Estevez, and Magaloni 2016; Boix 2019; Iversen and Soskice 2019). Another tradition focuses on the evolution and variation in laws and norms to explain a host of policies and practices related to the distribution of economic growth, social insurance, labor policy and other features of capitalist democracies (e.g., Olson 1982; Iversen 2005; Greif 2006; Mares 2006; North, Wallis, and Weingast 2009; Besley and Persson 2011; Fukuyama 2011; Stasavage 2011; Acemoglu and Robinson 2012; Beramendi 2012; Bates 2017).

On-going theoretical and empirical breakthroughs in understanding political economic processes provide the basis for rethinking how we can and how we should reinvent both the politics and economies of capitalist democracies. They inform ideas for redesigning political institutions, a topic to which we now turn. They also are critical to the development of some of the new frameworks we discuss in the concluding section of this Element.

3 Behavior, Cooperation, and Governance

In Section 2, we followed the rise and fall of political economic frameworks from the nineteenth to the twenty-first century. We saw how political economic frameworks are neither written in stone nor immutable. They are, instead, the product of moral and political choices that social actors make and remake.

It is time to make new choices. Our goal is to strengthen modern capitalist democracies' ability to ensure the well-being of humans and the environment.

---

[28] See, e.g., Iversen (1999), Mares (2003), and Thelen (2004).

This requires responding to massive challenges, such as inequality and climate change. It also requires responding to the rise of new, powerful vested interests produced by transformations in the economy – most notably, private and corporate actors in the realms of technology and finance. Tackling these challenges, we argue, entails designing and redesigning governance structures to better engender democratic capabilities, relational equality, and inclusive, expanded communities of fate.

A fresh reading of the social scientific research on human behavior and cooperation provides guidance for the design process. What we know about human behavior shapes how we define the possibilities and limits of cooperation and, ultimately, of governance. We thus focus on the microfoundations of governance – how humans successfully cooperate with one another and govern themselves in the absence of a third-party rule-maker and enforcer.[29] Our goal is to use the science of cooperation and self-governance to engineer inclusive participatory spaces that can fit within the existing representative structures of modern capitalist democracies. These spaces can improve democratic governance and check the power of vested interests by fostering participation, limiting hierarchy, and diffusing power.

Our account begins with a simple premise: humans are inherently social creatures. Aristotle famously likened the social nature of humans to that of "other gregarious animals" (Aristotle 1995 [335–323 BCE], book 1). Like bees and ants, humans have a tendency to cooperate. But Aristotle was no fool. He understood, as do the contemporary social scientists we consider here, that human sociality does not mean that cooperation is effortless.

In this section we provide evidence that challenges two presumptions about cooperation that seem prima facie incontrovertible: cooperation is easy in small groups and hierarchy is the best way to promote cooperation at scale. We sift through a vast literature that spans a number of academic fields – from sociobiology to communication – and ranges across different forms of human organization, from hunter-gatherer bands to online communities. We analyze the institutional arrangements that facilitate cooperation at multiple scales in the absence of hierarchical structures of control. In other words, we study the arrangements that facilitate self-governance.

The scope of our investigation allows us to embrace a broad definition of self-governance. When we speak of self-governance today, we often refer to the structure of representative government associated with modern liberal democracy. But because this structure is what we ultimately hope to redesign, we also

---

[29] Although they differ in some respects, here we use the notions of cooperation and self-governance interchangeably.

look at a variety of instances that broaden our imagination of what is possible. Some of our cases explore self-governing arrangements that emerged in the shadow of a formal government – liberal or otherwise. Others explore self-governing arrangements that emerged long before formal governments even developed.

The evidence shows that no matter the size of the group – tiny or huge – and its purpose – survival or entertainment – self-governance works better when institutions exist to 1) allow members to collectively articulate and amend the rules, and 2) define and enforce appropriate forms of redress for those who misbehave. Moreover, the still-limited research on inclusive self-governance also suggests that, by fostering strong leadership, shared norms, and well-designed selection, deliberation, and decision-making mechanisms, we can offset self-governance's exclusive tendencies and build inclusive, expanded communities of fate.

Two objections to a more participatory democracy can be raised at the outset. First, it is a waste of time (at best) and counterproductive (at worst) to engage "the people" in governance because people are lazy and ignorant. If they could be bothered to show up and try, they would design the rules that best suit their particularistic interests, disregarding the needs of others. This objection, or strands thereof, is often associated with John Stuart Mill and features in many modern articulations of elitist democracy from Joseph Schumpeter's (1942) to Jason Brennan's (2016). But it is in fact as old as democracy itself: the Athenian historian Thucydides (2013) famously regarded his fellow citizens as an ignorant mob and thought that the city's democracy could only survive as long as its capable leader, Pericles, was around. Of course, the Athenian democracy survived and prospered for over one hundred years after Pericles' death, notably by strengthening its participatory institutions (Carugati 2019). Second, even if structures for self-governance could be designed to incentivize people to show up, try harder, and be a little more other-regarding, they would not be as effective as either having an enlightened elite or a Leviathan. This objection is famously associated with the work of Plato and Hobbes and continues to inform the thinking of political economists.

The goal of our investigation is to show that there is another way. In this section, we establish proof of concept for structures of self-governance that are based on more realistic assumptions about human behavior and the possibilities and limits of cooperation; that are compatible with values we cherish; and that can help us sustain expanded communities of fate. Our cases show that structures of self-governance exist at all scales and for many different purposes. Often, these structures do a more-than-decent job in achieving the group's goals. If not always superior to their hierarchical counterparts in terms of performance, such structures embody other important values, including voice, participation, and relational equality.

We do not wish to suggest that institutional arrangements that embrace these values are the best for all circumstances. We do not deny that scale and participation involve a tradeoff: establishing channels for meaningful participation becomes very difficult when many people are involved and when they are geographically dispersed. Recognizing this tradeoff does not, however, imply that representation and participation are mutually exclusive. Many of the theorists we discuss in this section have grappled with the tension between participation and scale and offered different solutions, notably Weingast on federalism (1995) and Ostrom on polycentric governance (2010a). But, we suggest, a robust science of participation is still in its infancy. Its development requires more rigorous delineation of: 1) the conditions for making self-governance and participation truly inclusive, 2) when participatory structures are needed or desirable and when instead they might be counterproductive and representation preferable, and 3) how to build effective participatory structures compatible with today's representative democracies.

Representation has enabled democracy to operate at an unprecedented scale. But as we strengthened representative institutions, we lost sight of the people whose interests these institutions are meant to embody and protect. The erasure of participatory spaces happened in part by design, as the product of a theory of human behavior that is skeptical of people's abilities to govern themselves (as we saw above). At the same time, we have also lost the rich texture of civic associations that Alexis de Tocqueville so highly regarded and that has been linked to democratic performance (Tocqueville 1990 [1835]; Putnam 1993; Skocpol 2003). As a result, all we have left is a tenuous link with the spaces where decisions are made and the people who make those decisions.[30]

Writing in the summer of 2020, in the midst of a pandemic that could not muffle the masked voices of a global intersectional social justice movement, we see our claims about the need to strengthen participation reflected in the streets. These are the voices of people long ignored and demanding to be heard and to have their concerns reflected in policy and government practices. Their most effective form of voice is protest. New institutional arrangements ought to be created to address these legitimate appeals for inclusion in a political system that calls itself democratic. In this section, we begin to delineate how we can design these arrangements.

---

[30] We are hardly alone in both decrying the decline in civic associations and searching for correctives. It is a rich and growing literature. See, for example, Putnam (2000), Fung (2006), Klinenberg (2018), Rahman and Gilman (2019), Commission on the Practice of Democratic Citizenship (2020), and Putnam and Garrett (2020).

Self-governance: An Interdisciplinary Overview

We begin with the insights from studies of cooperation and self-governance at small and medium scale. By presenting relatively simpler empirical settings, these studies offer important insights that are usually harder to capture in larger and more complex ones (Ostrom 1990, 27; Diamond 2012, 6–9; Ahlquist and Levi 2013, 10–12, chapter. 9; Ober 2015, 25–8; Carugati 2019, 9–10). If it is often said that small scale facilitates cooperation, these cases show that small scale does not make cooperation effortless. We then consider some exciting new work on cooperation at larger scales, including the largest-scale community of all – the one created by the internet.

Before we begin, a caveat: it is difficult and ultimately arbitrary to place hard boundaries around the definitions of small, medium, or large scale. But for the purpose of this section, "small-scale" communities are small enough that the interactions among their members are mostly face-to-face. Face-to-face means not just that interactions take place without the use of mediating technology but also, and perhaps more importantly, that people know each other; in numerical terms, these are "societies of hundreds" (Diamond 2012,14). Examples of small-scale human communities are hunter-gatherer societies. In medium-scale communities, whose members number in the thousands, people often don't know each other; these include, for example, some of the communities managing common pool resources. Finally, large-scale communities involve people that mostly don't know each other and have no obvious reason to cooperate, such as the members of online communities.

(Very) Small Scale: Hunter-Gatherers

Even when the scale of the group is very small and individuals have strong incentives to cooperate, such as blood ties and the need to survive, cooperation is not easy. Studying prehistoric hunter-gatherers and modern tribesmen, the cultural anthropologist and primatologist Christopher Boehm (1999, 12) suggests that cooperation in small groups is, "the product of human intentionality" and a constant hard-fought battle against domination.[31] For Boehm, egalitarian cooperation is not the absence, or the opposite, of hierarchy. Instead, it is hierarchy turned on its head: it is the "hierarchy of the rank and file" who band together to protect each other from those who might deem themselves more equal than others.

This battle against domination is made easier by the presence of what Boehm calls "an egalitarian ethos," that is, "strongly held moralistic positions about

---

[31] Boehm's theory of egalitarianism, it is worth noting, applies to adult men.

how life should be" (Boehm 1999, 68). This ethos is not a fuzzy normative construct. Rather, it is a set of highly practical solutions to problems the group habitually faces. These include aversion to hierarchy and wealth accumulation, consensus-seeking decision-making practices, and the oft-cited ladder of forms of redress for misbehavior, from mockery to assassination (Diamond 2012; Morris, Seaford, and Macedo 2015, chapter 2). Moreover, for Boehm (1999, 8), egalitarian societies "are created and maintained by moral communities" which "judge the doings of others ... decide that an individual is ... in need of sanctioning ... [and] engage in ridicule or other forms of direct social pressure – and in ostracism, for this work is done by a well-catalyzed group that must be in broad agreement if it is to act effectively." Conformity and sanctioning, then, are the key to successful cooperation in small groups.

Boehm's work thus suggests that a community's small scale is not, in and of itself, a guarantee of successful cooperation among its members.[32] Indeed, even in small hunter-gatherer communities, maintaining cooperative behaviors necessary to the survival of the moral community is quite difficult: it requires constant monitoring of upstarts and costly punishment, and the maintenance of agreement on what constitutes wrongdoing and how to properly treat those who misbehave. When humans cooperate in small groups, cooperation is made easier by the existence of shared norms regulating behavior to efficiently solve habitual problems.

Small(ish) Scale: Interest Groups

Concerns about cooperation in small groups do not only arise among prehistoric hunter-gatherers. Arguing against the view that cooperation is a given when people have interests in common, Mancur Olson (1965) documented the importance of the free rider problem as an obstacle to cooperation in the provision of public goods, that is, goods that are non-excludable and non-rivalrous.[33] Free riding results from the rational calculation that a person can share in the public good without contributing to it. However, if enough people free ride, the public good will not be provided at all. Deterrence of free riding requires that the right incentive structures are in place. These include selective incentives, that is, targeted rewards for participation or punishment for non-contributors.

---

[32] Indeed, rates of violence among hunter-gatherers, in prehistory as well in modern times, are appallingly high (Morris, Seaford, and Macedo 2015), even though in many cases violence is directed against upstarts, which is paradoxically a sign of successful group cooperation.

[33] Non-excludable and non-rivalrous mean that it is impossible to exclude others from use, and that consumption by one user does not reduce overall consumption.

Free riding undermines relational equality. It can also be conceptualized as a form of veto power, hindering the goals the majority seek. The problem exists in groups of all sizes, although it becomes more severe as group size increases. Overcoming the free rider problem is also a basis for power by making possible the creation of an organization that enables a group of individuals to make collective demands. In some instances, such as workers' unions, those who lacked bargaining power can gain it and escape from certain forms of domination. In other instances, for example the cartels created by oil-rich countries, overcoming free riding can further enhance the economic and political power of the already powerful to dominate a market and its consumers.

Getting Larger: Ostrom's CPR Communities

The tragedy of the commons refers to the overuse of a shared-resource system, such as a pasture or a fishing ground, by individuals acting in their own rational self-interest (Hardin 1968). Economists, political scientists, and policy wonks all believed that only markets and (Leviathan-style) states could provide effective governance structures to mitigate the tragedy. They were mistaken. Political scientist Elinor Ostrom showed instead that, under a given set of circumstances, self-governing groups could successfully manage common pool resources (CPRs)[34] – and, in some cases, do so for a long time. The groups Ostrom studied were located all over the world, spanning a dizzying array of cultures, languages, and traditions, and ranging from very small communities of 100 fishers in Turkey to the inhabitants of Japanese rural villages numbering in the thousands.

Ostrom still relied on the rational model of human behavior that underpins neoclassical economics. But she also challenged it by pointing out, simply and elegantly, the problems of transferring the model's theoretical simplifications to more complex empirical settings and, most dangerously, of using such simplifications to derive policy implications (Ostrom 1990, 6, 22–3).

Arguably, her major contribution was the development of eight design principles for self-governance in CPRs. These include, "clearly defined boundaries, congruence between [. . .] rules and the local conditions, collective-choice arrangements, monitoring, graduated sanctions, conflict-resolution mechanisms, [. . .] recognition of rights to organize, [and for larger CPRs] nested enterprises" (Ostrom 1990, 90–1). These principles facilitate important democratic capabilities, such as participation and the exercise of voice, and they

---

[34] The technical definition of CPR is a resource that is non-excludable and rivalrous. This means that it is costly to exclude others from use, and that consumption by one user reduces overall consumption.

contribute to freedom from domination, and relational equality. Indeed, the principles demonstrate how these values are compatible with effective self-governance, at least in CPR communities.

Ostrom's principles bear striking similarities with the strategies we already saw in earlier sections, and particularly in Boehm's work on hunter-gatherers: successful cooperation requires clear rules, mutual monitoring, dispute resolution, and punishment, and spaces for the collective articulation and amendment of those institutions and the normative principles underpinning them. These principles can foster effective self-governance while preventing the formation of hierarchy and the accumulation of power in the hands of a few.

Do these strategies apply beyond hunter-gatherer societies, interest groups, and CPRs? Indeed, the principles apply to a common set of problems faced in all collective-action situations. As such, they have influenced studies of self-governance in settings as remote from CPRs as online communities. Ostrom's frameworks for institutional analysis and development (IAD) and socio-ecological systems (SES) projected the principles beyond the study of CPRs and inspired generations of scholars concerned with protecting natural resources and the earth all the way up to those resources that require cooperation at a global level (Kinzig, Ehrlich, Alston, Arrow, Barrett, Buchman, Daily, Levin, Levin, Oppenheimer, Ostrom, and Saari 2013).

Governance in the Shadow of the State: Private Ordering

Boehm's hunter-gatherers and many of Ostrom's CPR communities existed in the absence, or removed from the reach, of a centralized government. One may assume, then, that once the state appears, the principles for effective decentralized cooperation and self-governance must yield. The literature on "private ordering" – that is, legal orders emerging from interactions among private actors – shows instead that the principles continue to shape cooperative strategies in communities operating within, albeit sometimes in the shadow or in defiance of, the central state. In addition, this literature emphasizes the importance of legal structures for rule-making and enforcement – structures that can coexist with a state's formal legal system, while providing more efficient or, as we will see in a moment, more suitable outcomes for the members of the community. Finally, the literature as a whole shows how broadly applicable the principles are, as it covers a wide array of different groups, with different purposes, and in different historical periods. These include, to name just a few, cattle ranchers in Shasta County, California, in the 1980s (Ellickson 1991), the international diamond industry (Bernstein 1992; Richman 2017), California gold rushers (Clay and Wright 2005), and medieval merchants in Europe and the Maghreb (Greif 1989; Milgrom, North, and Weingast 1990; Greif 1994, 2006).[35]

Take, for example, Lisa Bernstein's study of the diamond industry. The diamond industry might be perceived as the epitome of the kind of relatively small, exclusive, and cohesive community where size and homogeneity facilitate effective cooperation. Yet, according to Bernstein, even among diamantaires self-governance requires complex arrangements. In fact, the industry "developed an elaborate, internal set of rules, complete with distinctive institutions and sanctions, to handle disputes among industry members" (Bernstein 1992, 115). These include handshakes, spoken words, distinctively folded envelopes, and a whole private arbitration system. Arguing against the common view that private ordering institutions emerge primarily to lower the transaction costs of entering a legally enforceable contract, Bernstein suggests that other factors played a role. In particular, the diamond industry highly valued the secrecy of trade practices (1992, 116, 124), supported by strong reputational bonds.[36] By adapting these processes, the industry was able to organize itself as a powerful cartel protecting a very lucrative trade.

Drawing extensively from the private ordering literature, and abstracting from each individual case, Gillian Hadfield and Barry Weingast (2012, 2013, 2014) articulated a model of decentralized order that breaks down the often fictitious barrier between formal and informal legal institutions. The model shows how a distinctively legal order can emerge and be sustained in the absence of formal, centralized state institutions. Rules must display attributes that echo the legal philosophy literature, including clarity, transparency, consistency and so on (see, e.g., Hayek 1944, 1960; Fuller 1965). The rules are under the control of what the authors call an "authoritative steward," an identifiable entity that provides a unique normative classification of behavior. In order to promote effective decentralized enforcement, the classification must be common knowledge, meaning that each member knows that the others know the rules of accepted behavior. The classification must also be incentive-compatible, meaning that the incentives for an action must offset the costs of the action.

---

[35] It is important to mention that, for some of these cases, heated debates are ongoing concerning the relationship between, and relative role of, centralized and decentralized institutions, e.g., Edwards and Ogilvie (2008), Goldberg (2012), and Kadens (2015).

[36] Bernstein's work on the diamond industry, like much of the private ordering literature, also reveals the importance of repeat interactions, as well as mechanisms such as trustworthiness and reputation that may be built through such interactions. These principles have received ample treatment well beyond the private ordering literature. On repeat interactions, see, e.g., Axelrod (1984). On trust, trustworthiness, and reputation, see Levi and Stoker (2000), Hardin (2002), Cook, Hardin, and Levi (2005), and Levi (2019).

The private ordering literature emphasizes principles that foster democratic capabilities and relational equality by distributing power and limiting hierarchy. These include shared and clear norms of behavior, common spaces to articulate and debate those norms, and institutions for monitoring and sanctioning. But the private ordering literature also contributes to a more thorough understanding of the attributes that effective rules and mechanisms must display: these include attributes often associated with the concept of rule of law, as well as common knowledge and incentive-compatibility. As we will see in the next section, these principles continue to operate even when the size of the group increases dramatically.

Large like a (Small) State: Premodern Europe and Beyond

Premodern states present a unique advantage: they offer a window into the dynamics of self-governance at the level of the state, but without the structures that characterize modern capitalist democracies. As such, they enrich our understanding of how to build and sustain self-governance arrangements at larger scales.

Much work on premodern European states emphasizes the importance of credible commitments and self-enforcing rules for the emergence and sustainability of limited governments in early modern republics, including Venice, Genoa, and the United States (Weingast 1997; Greif and Laitin 2004; González de Lara, Greif, and Jha 2008; Mittal and Weingast 2013).

Focusing on the 1,000+ city-states (*poleis*) of ancient Greece, the historian and political theorist Josiah Ober (2015) focused on the role of information.[37] For Ober, the success of the Greeks' decentralized governance structures depended on institutions that enabled autonomous and diverse individuals to freely exchange and effectively aggregate information.[38] Effectively aggregated dispersed knowledge ensures that a diversity of perspectives is considered, and common knowledge of these perspectives facilitates alignment. Together, aggregation and alignment make the group better than the sum of its

---

[37] Section 2 showed how the rational theory of behavior assumed complete information by all actors in the exchange, until the assumption was effectively challenged in the 1970s and 1980s. Since then, a significant amount of scholarship has focused on the role of information for organizational performance, particularly in knowledge-based enterprises (Benkler 2002; Farrell and Schneier 2018). Information, it turns out, is critical to the comparative advantage of self-governing structures relative to their hierarchical counterparts.

[38] Not all poleis featured egalitarian institutions domestically. Even though the data reveals a clear trend in the spread of democracy by the fourth century BCE (Teegarden 2014), some poleis were run by oligarchs (Simonton 2019). But as an ecology, the Greek city-states display a remarkable level of what Ober refers to as "dispersed authority" (Ober 2015).

parts (as in Aristotle's famous potluck in *Politics* [3.1281a42-b10]; cf. Landemore and Elster 2012; Landemore 2013).

In Athens, the best documented of all the poleis, institutions capable of effectively eliciting and aggregating dispersed knowledge enabled large-scale participation in decision-making by the entire adult male population, relational equality among these actors, and forms of dignity extended beyond the citizen body to noncitizens and even to slaves (Ober 2012, 2008). Although we might assume that the citizens of Athens acted as a powerful interest group that defined and enforced the rules to benefit the members of the community to the detriment of outsiders, the evidence reveals that, over time, Athenian self-governing institutions evolved to include new actors. The evolution, driven by economic concerns, benefited the citizens – by bringing much-needed human and capital resources to the city – as much is it benefited the new actors, especially by protecting their right to property and contract enforcement, and by extending freedoms of religion and association (Carugati, Hadfield, and Weingast 2015; Carugati 2019, 2020b).

Broadening considerably the scope of the investigation into premodern self-governance, David Stasavage's recent book provides powerful evidence for the feasibility of scalable self-governing structures beyond the well-known cases of early-modern Europe and ancient Greece. Stasavage suggests that early democracy, understood as "a system in which a ruler governed jointly with a council or assembly composed of members of society who were themselves independent from the ruler and not subject to his or her whim" (Stasavage 2020, 4–5), was a common form of governance in many parts of the world. No ruler can ever govern alone, but Stasavage's account shows that the fundamental distinction between early democracies and early autocracies revolved around whether the ruler's coalition was organized as an independent body capable of checking his or her power, or as a bureaucracy under the ruler's control. The conditions for the development of early democracies and their independent councils included a polity's small scale, the lack of a strong, preexisting bureaucratic structure to assess and measure production, and the presence of exit options that would enable subjects to relocate elsewhere.

If, as Stasavage documents, early democracies were roughly as common as early autocracies (Stasavage, 2020, 5), then a body of still-understudied evidence is ripe for analysis. As we continue to develop the tools to explore this evidence, we will be able to test the robustness of the structures that emerge from the cases of early modern Europe and ancient Greece, including institutions for credible commitment, self-enforcing rules, and institutions enabling the aggregation and alignment of dispersed information. We will also surely learn more about the structures that make self-governance possible, or otherwise lead to its demise.

Longshore Unions ... in the Interest of Others

The skeptic may point out that all the groups we have reviewed so far had plenty of good reasons to cooperate. Hunter-gatherers were tied by blood, and cooperation was the only means to avoid widespread violence and death. Interest groups owe their very existence to the pursuit of a common interest. Communities managing common pool resources depended on the resource for their livelihood, and the same can be said for the diamond traders discussed in the private ordering literature. Even the citizens of early democracies, including Athens and the early modern European republics were, after all, members of the same polity striving to avoid hierarchy and domination.

Yet, some research exists suggesting that the principles we have identified so far in this section extend to groups with no apparent reasons to cooperate. John Ahlquist and Margaret Levi (2013) investigated the case of longshore union members in the United States and Australia who engaged in port closures and other job actions in support of faraway strangers involved in social justice struggles. The case of the longshore unions enables us to take a step beyond principles that characterize a community of self-governing agents toward inclusive participatory structures where cooperation operates, as Ahlquist and Levi put it, *in the interest of others*.

They asked: What motivates members of a union, designed to meet their material needs, to engage in costly actions on behalf of a wider community? Ahlquist and Levi found that some organizational structures do not merely facilitate the aggregation of individual preferences. Conversely, they transform preferences.[39]

In these unions, highly accountable leaders successfully delivered what their members rightfully expect of unions: better wages and working conditions, job security and safety, and social insurance. But the union also introduced members to events in the world and then allowed them to come to a determination about whether and how to act. It was built on democratic processes that allowed for discussion and confirmation of information about atrocities and for voting for the appropriate actions to take. A critical part of the formula was the constitution of democratic institutions that encouraged challenges to leadership and expression of voice. Equally important were the norms of fairness, solidarity, and shared destiny with others that defined the common ethos of these unions.

---

[39] For a similar argument about organizations transforming members by developing their capacity for organizing and leadership, see Han (2014).

Through a combination of socialization and civic education, the members came to believe that they had an obligation to defend against violations of human rights across the globe, even when that obligation required personally costly actions on behalf of strangers. They came to believe that if you tolerated injustices against populations anywhere, you opened the floodgates to the possibility of rights abuses everywhere. In the words of the legendary Knights of Labor and later the Industrial Workers of the World: "An injury to one is an injury to all." This is the slogan adopted by the International Longshore and Warehouse Workers Union (ILWU), one of the principal unions in the study.

In sum, institutional structures that promoted the creation of these expanded communities of fate included transparent and accountable leadership, as well as institutions that provided equal opportunity for political influence through votes and persuasive argument, and which offered education to their members about the political, social, and economic context in which choices were made. As a result, members of these communities came to be driven, among other things, by a form of farsighted altruism which enabled them to make costly sacrifices on behalf of those with whom they believed their fates, and their descendants' fates, were entwined but who may never be able to directly reciprocate.

It is this type of community that we hope to engineer again and again wherever acting "in the interest of others" yields improvements in human and environmental well-being. Before we wrap up our interdisciplinary overview to draw some design principles for fostering democratic capabilities, relational equality, and inclusive communities of fate, one last case deserves mention for the promise it holds to expand our knowledge of self-governance institutions: that of online communities.

Going Digital: Online Communities

If the neoclassical rational model of behavior applied, Wikipedia would not exist. As Benkler, Shaw, and Hill put it, "the rise of networked systems and online platforms for collective intelligence has upended many of the assumptions and findings from this earlier research" (Benkler, Shaw, and Hill 2015, 2). Neither contracts and ownership, nor hierarchy and management can fully explain the large number of decentralized volunteer contributors to one of the largest collaborative projects the world has ever seen. At the same time, the authors continue, "online collective intelligence systems have generated data sources for the study of social organization and behavior at unprecedented scale and granularity." Wikipedia is perhaps the most famous and well-studied but certainly not the only case (Benkler, Shaw, and Hill 2015, 3).

Early studies of peer production celebrated its decentralized organization, lack of material incentives, and high-quality products (Benkler 2002). But a new generation of scholars steeped in the language of organizational and institutional studies has now tempered the initial optimism, producing more nuanced analyses. Many scholars have analyzed online communities' governance structures, documenting the existence of hierarchies, bureaucracies, and inequality (Kittur, Chi, Pendleton, Suh, and Mytkowicz 2007; Butler, Joyce, and Pike 2008; Shaw and Hill 2014; Schneider 2019). These structures have been linked to performance decline. For example, in an influential study of Wikipedia, replicated for 740 Wikis by TeBlunthuis, Shaw, and Hill (2018), Halfaker and colleagues (Halfaker, Geiger, Morgan, and Riedl 2012) suggest that the decline in the number of contributors is due to norm entrenchment.

Much of this literature confirms findings from studies of offline cooperation: size matters, and communication, group structure, and rules and regulations help avoid conflict (Kittur and Kraut 2010). Interestingly, the authors suggest that different mechanisms operate at different scales with policies and regulations operating when groups are small and the other mechanisms operating at larger scales. However, these studies have at times yielded findings that challenge previous literature on cooperation, online and offline. For example, in a recent paper, Narayan and colleagues (Narayan, TeBlunthuis, Hale, Hill, and Shaw 2019) find that facilitating interpersonal communication among wiki contributors does not yield increased productivity and hinders participation.

The study of online cooperation and self-governance is one the many frontiers of organizational studies for at least three reasons. First, it offers a new and remarkable opportunity to study large-scale cooperation. Second, as Benkler, Shaw and Hill suggested, it enables us to test current theories of cooperation and governance, and the behavioral assumptions on which they are based. And finally, it makes possible to study almost in real-time the processes of experimentation that may yield new and robust structures, or make them less resilient or scalable.

However, as this section suggests, online collective intelligence systems are not the only cases of self-governance arrangements that can teach us something about the possibilities and limits of cooperation. Indeed, reading all these cases together will be crucial to developing a new science of self-governance.[40]

---

[40] Carugati (2020a) makes a similar argument about comparing the evidence from premodern societies and online communities.

Design Principles for Institution-Building

In the previous section, we offered an interdisciplinary overview of the literature on cooperation and self-governance to identify some principles that can help us strengthen the fraying structure of modern capitalist democracy. Our investigation suggests that self-governance arrangements at all scales are possible, can be effective, and may display morally desirable attributes, such as relational equality, voice, and participation. Moreover, robust self-governing arrangements are those whose participants can collectively articulate and amend the rules and define and enforce appropriate forms of redress for those who misbehave. Additional strategies for successful self-governance include shared norms with normatively desirable attributes, education about the context in which choices are made, free exchange and effective aggregation of information, and transparent and accountable leadership. Some of these structures are capable of sustaining not just self-governance in exclusive communities, but also cooperation in more inclusive, expanded communities of fate.

The evidence for this type of inclusive cooperative community, however, is rather limited. To further illustrate how the design principles may operate in practice to strengthen self-governance, foster relational equality, and check the power of vested interest in today's capitalist democracies, we engage in a thought experiment.

✳ *A Council for Algorithms*

In this section, we use the principles to imagine how we can better govern one of the most powerful vested interests of third-millennium capitalist democracies: the technology sector. In particular, we suggest how we might create a new institution to tackle the governance challenge of regulating the use of algorithms in society. The need to improve algorithmic governance offers an opportunity to diffuse power and limit hierarchy in the ever-growing technology sector, while fostering democratic capabilities, relational equality and inclusive communities of fate among those called upon to make decisions about the use of algorithms in society.

Algorithms are, essentially, rule-based structures for making decisions. They have been around for a long time (for example, to evaluate risk for insurers). But a new generation of algorithms, those powered by machine learning, poses some difficult new challenges. First and foremost, these algorithms play an increasingly large role in our lives, suggesting what we should read and watch, whom we should date, and whether or not we are detained while awaiting trial. Second, although they hold great promise in some fields – for example, they can better detect cancers – they can also discriminate based on the color of our skin or the zip code we live in.[41] Yet, despite their ubiquity in society, no real structure exists to regulate algorithms' use.[42]

The Algorithmic Accountability Act, parked with the Committee on Energy and Commerce since its introduction in April 2019, "requires companies to study and fix flawed computer algorithms that result in inaccurate, unfair, biased or discriminatory decisions impacting Americans" (Booker 2019). The Act calls for impact assessments, as in the EU and Canadian versions. But it is debatable whether asking companies to conduct impact assessments is a sufficient response. On the one hand, researchers are pushing back against the use of algorithms in some institutions, for example, in the criminal justice system (Barabas, Virza, Dinakar, Ito, and Zittrain 2018; Mayson 2019). On the other hand, these systems are spreading in the public sector (Engstrom and Ho 2020). Researchers have also called for mechanisms to ensure due process (Citron 2007), avoid disparate impact (Barocas and Selbst 2016), and create recourse mechanisms (Alkhatib and Bernstein 2019). An interdisciplinary and intersectoral group of experts headed by researchers at the independent organization OpenAI (Brundage, Avin, Wang, Belfield, Krueger, Hadfield, Khlaaf, Yang, Toner, and Fong 2020) has recently suggested the creation of an external auditing body but did not specify what such a body should look like.

We don't know how to regulate algorithms, because their application to societal problems involves a fundamental incongruity. Algorithms follow logical rules in order to optimize for a given outcome. But much public policy is all a matter of tradeoffs: optimizing for some groups in society makes others worse off. Resolving social tradeoffs, for algorithms as well as for many other issues, requires that many different voices be heard. As such, the challenge of regulating algorithms may provide an opportunity to strengthen the kind of structures for fostering democratic capabilities, relational equality, and inclusive, expanded communities of fate that we studied in this section.

So how can we better govern algorithms? Although ours is a thought experiment, we don't need to engage in pure speculation to articulate a solution. We are guided by the principles and inspired by the case of one society that built its entire governance structure on the notion that people should have a voice and an equal say in decision-making – ancient Athens.

One Athenian institution provides a particularly useful model: the Council of Five Hundred, a deliberative body in charge of all decision-making, from war to

---

[41] Grady 2019. But see Kleinberg, Ludwig, Mullainathan, and Sunstein (2018) on the ease algorithms afford in *proving* discrimination, pushing scrutiny back to the design stage, and Sunstein (2019) on algorithms' ability to overcome cognitive biases.

[42] Independent resources to track the use of algorithms in society are multiplying (Engstrom and Ho 2020). Also, see these websites: https://algorithmwatch.org/en/ and https://pretrialrisk.com/.

state finance to entertainment. Every year, fifty Athenian citizens from each of the ten tribes were selected by lot to serve. Selection occurred among those that had not served the year before and had not already served twice. These simple organizational rules facilitated broad participation, knowledge aggregation, and citizen learning (Ober 2008). First, because the term was limited and could not be iterated more than twice, over time a broad section of the population – rich and poor, educated and not – participated in decision-making. Second, because the council represented the whole population (each tribe integrated three different geographic constituencies), it could draw upon the diverse knowledge of its members. Third, at the end of their mandate, councilors returned home with a body of knowledge about the affairs of their city that they could share with their families, friends, and coworkers, some of whom had already served and some who soon would. Certainly, the Athenians did not follow through on their commitment to inclusion. As a result, many people's voices went unheard, including those of women, foreigners, and slaves. But we don't need to follow the Athenian example on this front.

The Algorithmic Council uses the principles we outlined as essential to the design of new institutional arrangements in a new moral political economy. First, it creates a participatory space for deliberation and debate to articulate the rules and establish enforcement mechanisms. Second, as a permanent institution, it enables the type of institutional learning that is critical to amending the rules as circumstances, norms, and preferences change. Its members are randomly selected and in charge of decisions for a limited time, preventing the accumulation of power and fostering relational equality. Moreover, by design, the councilors are asked to embody the interests of a community that goes well beyond the given group of decision-makers, as their judgments will affect distant others, sometimes even in different countries. And, of course, by their very participation at the root of the decision-making process, the councilors have a chance to shape the regulatory process in ways that can help check the power of the technology companies that design and implement the algorithms.

Of course, articulating these basics norms of engagement is only the first step toward robust institutional design. Many other rules and norms would also have to be carefully designed. For example: Who is eligible to participate? What would councilors base their deliberations on? Would the council be an advisory or authoritative body? What issues would come under its purview? And, finally, why a new council? Can't we just repurpose an existing institution or leave it to the private sector to self-regulate? Let us begin.

A citizen council for algorithms modeled on the Athenian example would represent the entire polity or, in some cases, those affected by the outcome of the collective choice, if the two do not coincide. Citizens' deliberations would be informed by agency self-assessments (Reisman, Schultz, Crawford, and Whittaker 2018), and algorithmic impact statements (Selbst 2017) for decision systems used by government agencies, and internal auditing reports for industry (Raji, Smart, White, Mitchell, Gebru, Hutchinson, Smith-Loud, Theron, and Barnes 2020), as well as by reports from investigative journalists and civil society activists, whenever available (Reisman et al. 2018). Ideally, the council would act as an authoritative body or as an advisory board to an existing regulatory agency. It could evaluate a variety of issues including the level of privacy protection, the extent to (and methods by) which the systems were tested for safety, security, or ethical concerns, and the sources of data, labor, and other resources used.

Compared to the council, other proposed structures might be less effective or less compatible with desirable norms. In the private sector, some advocate for internal auditing mechanisms, which raise obvious concerns about conflicts of interest (Raji et al. 2020).[43] Another position is to rely on existing institutions, like notice-and-comment procedures and review by courts. But as legal experts suggest, courts are ill-suited to wrestle with the type of systemic considerations involved in the deployment of AI systems, and judges might lack technical expertise as well as capacity (Engstrom and Ho 2020). A dedicated technical oversight board would be subject to the shortcomings of technocratic solutions: it would limit democratic accountability and fail to draw on the experience of those who are impacted the most by the decisions (for a similar example, see Facebook's brand-new "Supreme Court"). Prospective benchmarking – a process whereby public agencies would scrutinize cases chosen at random to compare AI-assisted and human outcomes – would improve democratic accountability, but still limit the range of expertise and relevant knowledge informing the review process (Engstrom and Ho 2020). Compared to these structures, the council would be a fair and efficient response to the question of how to resolve the societal tradeoffs that algorithms create by expanding the range of possible solutions to societal problems, enhancing democratic account-ability, and fostering citizen participation and learning. There are, of course, many other issues to tackle if our thought experiment is to be taken seriously. But, for now, these reflections must suffice.

Is ours a pie-in-the-sky idea with no chance of implementation? Perhaps. But, abstracting from the specifics of our suggestion, we are heartened to observe that all around the world, academics, social entrepreneurs, and policymakers are working hard toward designing similar institutions. It is especially encouraging

---

[43] Internal audits are still important, especially to generate material for review, and the same applies to audits by automated third parties. See Etzioni and Li (2019).

to see that some of the design principles we highlighted in this section have already been adopted in many innovative attempts to create meaningful partici-pation at various levels of decision-making. These include experiments in deliberative democracy (such as participatory budgeting, deliberative polling, and online deliberative town halls), citizen assemblies (including the recent discussions about data sharing and climate change in the UK and France); citizen-run state-level institutions (like the California Citizens Redistricting Commission); and new political parties (for example, Podemos in Spain, the Five Star Movement in Italy, and Net Party in Argentina). Some of these experiments use crowdsourcing, which has also been used to resolve disputes (e.g., Online Dispute Resolution platforms), gather data (e.g., citizen science), produce new scientific discoveries (e.g., Polymath Project), and even set national-level fiscal policy (e.g., the Finance Ministry of Taiwan).[44]

This is a large and fast-growing field. Of particular note are those experi-ments that mobilize entire countries, ask citizens to weigh in on very high-stakes issues, and then translate popular demands into national policies. These include the crowdsourcing process that mobilized the population of Iceland to write a new national constitution in 2011, the citizen assemblies that led to constitutional amendments to legalize abortion and marriage equality in Ireland in 2015 and 2018, and the very recent creation of a permanent citizen council and citizen assembly in Belgium in 2019.

All these experiments harness the diverse knowledge of citizens and encourage problem-solving (which is a very different intellectual endeavor than merely stating a problem, as the academics reading this section know well). But they are also, by and large, one-off consultative processes and only a few have actually generated policies.[45] Our investigation suggests a step forward: asking citizens for their input is good for public policy and good for democracy, but citizen engagement must be ongoing and foster learning processes that enable citizens to articulate, apply and, when needed, even change the rules.

***

＊ In this section, we began to tackle the question of how we might design institutions for cooperation and self-governance capable of checking the power of vested interests and of fostering democratic capabilities, relational

---

[44] Some of these experiments take advantage of digital technology. As we have learned all too well, technology may liberate, but it may also be used to repress (cf. Harari 2018; Feldstein 2019; Steinberg, Loyle, and Carugati 2021). For a discussion of the pros and cons of digital technology in relationship to democracy see Bernholz, Landemore, and Reich (2021).

[45] Even in the case of Belgium, the new permanent institutions' mandate is limited to formulating recommendations (cf. Sgueo 2020).

equality, and inclusive, expanded communities of fate. In our thought experiment, we also suggested that participatory self-governance might be preferable to representation when a plurality of voices is needed to solve major societal tradeoffs. Throughout the section, we pointed out where institutions for effective cooperation and self-governance at scale might be compatible with the existence of centralized governments, be they modern representative capitalist democracies (as in the case of Bernstein's diamond dealers) or not (as in the premodern cases or some of Ostrom's CPR communities).

Our work suggests that it is possible, if certainly not easy, to build many different kinds of structures for participatory self-governance in today's democracies. Such structures can strengthen democracy and enable a much broader community to engage on important issues. But our work also suggests how complex it is to build those structures within current institutions of representative government. We also recognize how difficult it is to build structures that can foster truly inclusive, expanded communities of fate. In this respect, much work remains to be done. We hope this Element can provide some building blocks and a way forward.

Conclusion

> Only a crisis – actual or perceived – produces real change. When that crisis occurs, the actions that are taken depend on the ideas that are lying around.
> Milton and Rose Friedman (1962), *Capitalism and Freedom*

As we wrote this Element in the summer of 2020, the economic and public health crisis produced by the COVID-19 pandemic combined with the political and social crisis fueled by demands for racial justice and social protections. We wrote this conclusion in the week that saw the storming of the US Capitol by an angry mob of anti-democratic thugs, an event that shook the country but failed to stop the certification of the next president. These major blows to an already fraying political economic framework present an opportunity for change. To achieve a reconstruction of our economic, political, and social structures, we need leaders committed to a new approach with advisors, policies, and practices to match. But the leaders and policies will only be successful to the extent that they are informed by ideas suited to the era we are in.

This Element presents an argument for reframing our society's goals in terms of human and environmental well-being. We advocate for the promotion of relational equality and for the reaffirmation of fundamental democratic values, including voice, participation, and political equality, which in turn require a commitment to enhancing democratic capabilities among the entire population. It also requires building institutions that strengthen the mechanisms of accountability and the restraints on nondemocratic sources of power. The values of human and planetary flourishing, relational equality, and democracy depend on a well-functioning economy and a well-performing government.

Our contribution stems from the realization that what we strive for as a society changes over time, requiring our institutional arrangements to correspondingly change and conform. Existing rules and regulations affecting markets, financial institutions, and corporations were written for a different era. Our model of government and many of the inherited aspects of representative democracy no longer serve our collective interests. Our physical and social infrastructure need rebuilding. The values we have emphasized and the ideas we have explored offer some guidance to reform our institutions, laws, norms, and social practices.

We have also insisted throughout that a political economic framework must incorporate political as well as economic analysis and concerns. That implies not only attention to the role of government but also an understanding of how institutional arrangements enhance the power of some and block or suppress the power of others. Emphasizing the political in political economy further clarifies how the distribution and allocation of wealth, the primary concern of economists, remains a question for political contestation and resolution.

The guidance we attempt to provide for institutional redesign rests on a series of claims. The first is that economies reflect moral and political choices. The second is that a political economic framework depends on assumptions about human motivations and rationality. We can no longer assume the rational individual of neoclassical economics, nor even the boundedly rational individual of behavioral economics. At the heart of all proposed new frameworks consistent with the values we promote is a social creature who cares about herself but also cares about and is connected to others through networks and communities of fate. Her ability to make decisions is influenced by systematic biases, emotions, and societally generated norms, and by those with whom she interacts. This individual is *homo reciprocans* (Bowles and Gintis 2002) or *sapiens integra* (Cottam and Slaughter 2020), embedded in networks both narrow and encompassing. She is capable of producing an expanded and inclusive community of fate – but only if our institutions support and assist the achievement of such a community.

Our third claim builds on something we have known for a long time: groups big and small must develop institutions to ensure that members play by the rules and that there are appropriate redress options available and enforceable, if and when they don't. Moreover, the design of those institutions must be grounded in our revised assumptions about human motivation and rationality if they are to effectively encourage certain actions and discourage others. What we critically add to these insights is how such institutional arrangements are most effective – and most democratic – when they enable participants to debate, articulate, and change the rules and means of enforcement. By fostering ongoing learning processes and experimentation within the polity, we can make democracy more robust, more inclusive, and more supportive of relational equality.

Modern democracy requires representative structures to cope with the sheer scale of today's nations. But, as we argued in Section 3, if scale and participation involve a tradeoff, it does not follow that representation and participation are mutually exclusive. To achieve a democracy that balances representation and participation is a design challenge. We know some of the principles. Participatory structures should evoke our prosocial nature, enable us to learn from and about each other, incorporate the possibilities as well as limits of human cooperation, and foster forms of engagement that are inclusive and enduring. Representative structures should facilitate flows of feedback and information, and they should have mechanisms to inhibit control by powerful interests. This requires providing voice and engagement at the points in the political process that inform the representatives' actions. However, it is not just a question of testimony; it is also a matter of engagement and knowledge-sharing between the various actors involved. And these interactions should not just be for show but should lead to better policies, better government officials, and better citizens. For example, when the issue is domestic abuse, the experts should encompass those who have experienced abuse, not only those who study the problem or are hired to help the victim. This was the strategy used by then-Senator Biden in 1990 as the chair of the US Senate hearings on the Violence against Women Act (United States 1990). The result was a far better law, attentive to the actual needs of those it was meant to serve.

By facilitating debate and contestation that recognizes and validates the concerns of all, it may be possible to reconstitute mutual respect and tolerance within our polities. By creating modes of decision-making that enable today's losers to feel their views have had a hearing and that they have a realistic chance for future wins, it may be possible to have a more civil politics. And it is these kinds of structures that can create and sustain expanded communities of fate.

As we build the path forward, we need ideas. And many ideas are now emerging at both the theoretical and practical policy levels. The most exciting new work in political economy advocates substituting aggregate economic growth with metrics based on measures of well-being and social justice and with an emphasis on the health of the planet as well as the health of society. These analyses incorporate issues of power, social cohesion, law, and ethics and suggest strategies for changing our contemporary practices in government and the economy. They evidence a deep grasp of human motivations, rationality, behavior, and institutions, and they people their models with humans who care about each other, reciprocate, and engage in complex networks of interaction. They are providing the ideas and tools essential to the construction of a new moral political economic framework.

The theoretical breakthroughs and empirical grasp we now have of political economic processes provide the basis for rethinking how we can and how we should reinvent both the politics and economies of capitalist democracies. A few examples will have to suffice from among the growing body of work.[46] Kate Raworth's best-selling *Doughnut Economics* (Raworth 2017) begins with the premise that it is possible to structure an economy and revise economics to meet the needs of people and the planet. She builds a model that presumes, first, a social foundation that inhibits human deprivation and, second, an ecological ceiling beyond which is planetary degradation. Wendy Carlin and Sam Bowles (2020) model the relationship among government, markets, and civil society to lay the groundwork for a new paradigm that takes into account power relationships. They emphasize how the "pursuit of a broader concept of freedom and the cultivation of the associated norms of solidarity, fairness, reciprocity, and sustainability would enhance the functioning of a successful modern economy" (Carlin and Bowles 2020, 377). Torben Iversen and David Soskice (2019) put their faith in the knowledge economy. They argue that capitalist democracy's empowerment of educated and skilled workers has in the past and will again produce an electoral base that will create pressure for policies that can lead to a better and more equitable capitalism. Danielle Allen offers an approach to reframing our political and economic institutions according to criteria that contribute to human flourishing. She argues for "empowering economies" that provide for material well-being, enhance productive capacity while making it free of domination, require democratic steering of the economy, and are grounded in rules that protect equal basic liberties (Allen forthcoming).

From this and related work are derived a plethora of programmatic ideas. The presidency of Joe Biden offers an opening for policy change in the United States, with potential worldwide impact. Several concrete examples of how this may play out include the basket of policies advocated by various members of the CASBS moral political economy network. Heather Boushey, a new member of the Council of Economic Advisors, argues for changes in education,

---

[46] See, e.g., Fung, Wright, and Abers (2003), Hacker and Pierson (2010), Wright (2010), Piketty (2014), Arthur (2015), Rodrik (2015), Jacobs and Mazzucato (2016), Streeck (2016), Page and Gilens (2017), Collier (2018), Posner and Weyl (2018), Boushey (2019), Rahman and Gilman (2019), Collier and Kay (2020), Cottam (2020), Henderson (2020), Piketty (2020), and Beinhocker and Hanauer (in progress).

regulation of the market, and many other domains that would enhance both social mobility and economic growth (Boushey 2019). Joshua Cohen presents the advantages of good jobs and the policies needed to achieve them, for example, higher minimum wages, better social protections, appropriate tax incentives to firms, and a significantly revised federal research and development (R&D) structure (Cohen 2020). Hilary Cottam offers an alternative to the welfare system in Britain and, by extension, to that in the United States (Cottam 2019). Colin Mayer (2018) and Rebecca Henderson (2020) each propose means to ensure purposeful corporations that take stakeholders – and the planet – into account in addition to shareholders.

There are also several proposals made by members of our network that are informed by the history and experience of marginalized groups, particularly Blacks. For example, there are arguments for federal job guarantees (Paul, Darity, and Hamilton 2018) and for reparations for the descendants of slaves (Darity and Mullen 2020). Freedom from domination and discrimination and freedom to develop capabilities are at the heart of these proposals.

Ideas do not have to come solely from academic circles. The Mont Pelerin Society, which we discussed in Section 2, provides an example. Validation by the media, by those who today we call influencers, by philanthropists, and, ultimately, by significant segments of the population were crucial to the spread and acceptance of the new classicals' ideas. The same applies today. Moreover, then, like now, it is helpful if new ideas are reinforced by the scholars on whose expertise policymakers would be calling.

Movements and their political entrepreneurs play a crucial role in communicating the new model of the world, and in policy advocacy. Some of the most effective social movements communicate not only injustice but also correctives. The living wage movement helped create a demand for an increased minimum wage and the marriage equality movement a transformation of the laws in the United States (Woodly 2015). A series of movements exposed the unavailability of adequate credit for marginalized groups and finally provoked federal government intervention in the housing market (Thurston 2018). When movements are successful, they constitute a countervailing power to vested interests, and they help structure the agenda of policymakers.

Sometimes the aims of movements and the agendas of political leaders sufficiently collide to change policy. A primary demand of the civil rights movement was protection of the Black franchise. Lyndon Baines Johnson acted in the interest of the commonweal to get the Civil Rights Act passed in 1964, even at the cost – as he foresaw – of the Southern Democrats defecting to the Republican Party. But not all such collisions are progressive. There are also examples where anti-tax, anti-government, and anti-left movements rely on political entrepreneurs to transform their demands into policy. President Reagan and President Trump are, in this respect, illustrative.

Ideas, movements, and sympathetic political leadership are only part of what is necessary to construct a new moral political economy. It is also essential to undermine the vested interests of those seeking to sustain the status quo. This involves more than the evolution of the economy; it also requires a political contest.

As we are all too well aware, this is a period of extraordinary ferment. We exist in a world of extreme oppositional perspectives about what concerns and whose concerns should be attended to, and there is real conflict over the very rules of the game. As in the 1930s, moments such as these can lead to progressive politics in one country and fascism in another. This Element has not addressed – and cannot address – what will ensure that the values of general human well-being, planetary survival, and relational equality will win out in this struggle, nor that democracy will prosper, let alone endure. Yet, we remain optimistic, and in that hope we contributed some ideas to ground a new and better framework for advancing our societal goals.

The stakes are high. In this crisis-ridden, white-water world, we need a refreshed democratic political economy more than ever. Thomas Jefferson is often misquoted as saying that we should have a revolution every generation. Our Element has a somewhat different prescription. Every generation should get a chance to review and assess how well the prevailing moral political economic framework is working and whether it fits with current societal values and goals – and to amend it if it does not. Political economic frameworks change with transformations in technology, knowledge, and trade. In the past, the molding of new frameworks has largely been the work of economists. In the future, we hope it is the work of an engaged citizenry drawing on their multiplicity of perspectives in a process that respects the verified facts and science essential to good decisions and robust institutional design.

References

Acemoglu, Daron, and James A. Robinson. 2006. *Economic Origins of Dictatorship and Democracy.* New York: Cambridge University Press.

——— 2012. *Why Nations Fail: The Origins of Power, Prosperity and Poverty.* New York: Crown Publishers.

Ahlquist, John S., and Margaret Levi. 2011. "Leadership: What It Means, What It Does, and What We Want to Know About It." *Annual Review of Political Science* 14 (1):1–24.

——— 2013. *In the Interests of Others: Leaders, Governance, and Political Activism in Membership Organizations.* Princeton, NJ: Princeton University Press.

Akerlof, George A. 1970. "The Market for 'Lemons': Quality Uncertainty and the Market Mechanism." *The Quarterly Journal of Economics* 84 (3):488–500.

Akerlof, George A., and Robert J. Schiller. 2010. *Animal Spirits: How Human Psychology Drives the Economy, and Why It Matters for Global Capitalism.* Princeton, NJ: Princeton University Press.

Alkhatib, Ali, and Michael Bernstein. 2019. "Street-Level Algorithms: A Theory at the Gaps between Policy and Decisions." https://hci .stanford.edu/publications/2019/streetlevelalgorithms/streetlevelalgo rithms-chi2019.pdf.

Allen, Danielle S. 2013. "A Connected Society." *Soundings* (53):103–13.

——— 2016. "Toward a Connected Society." In *Our Compelling Interests: The Value of Diversity for Democracy and a Prosperous Society*, ed. Earl Lewis and Nancy Cantor. Princeton, NJ: Princeton University Press.

——— 2020. "A New Theory of Justice: Difference without Domination." In *Difference without Domination*, ed. Danielle Allen and Rohini Somanathan. Chicago: University of Chicago Press.

——— Forthcoming. *Justice by Means of Democracy.* Chicago: University of Chicago.

Allen, Danielle S., and Rob Reich, eds. 2013. *Education, Justice, and Democracy.* Chicago: University of Chicago Press.

Amadae, S. M., and Bruce Bueno de Mesquita. 1999. "The Rochester School: The Origins of Positive Political Economy." *Annual Review of Political Science* 2:269–98.

Anderson, Elizabeth. 1993. *Value in Ethics and Economics.* Cambridge, MA.: Harvard University Press.

1999. "What is the Point of Equality?" *Ethics* 109 (2):287–337.

2010. "The Fundamental Disagreement between Luck Egalitarians and Relational Egalitarians." *Canadian Journal of Philosophy* 36:1–23.

2017. *Private Government: How Employers Rule Our Lives (and Why We Don't Talk about It)*, ed. Stephen Macedo. Princeton, NJ: Princeton University Press.

Ansell, Ben, and David Samuels. 2010. "Inequality and Democratization: A Contractarian Approach." *Comparative Political Studies* 43 (12):1543–74.

2014. *Inequality and Democratization: An Elite-Competition Approach.* New York: Cambridge University Press.

Aristotle. 1995 [335–323 BCE]. *Politics. Books I and II.* Oxford: Clarendon Press.

Arnott, Richard J., and Joseph E. Stiglitz. 1979. "Aggregate Land Rents, Expenditure on Public Goods, and Optimal City Size." *The Quarterly Journal of Economics* 93 (4):471–500.

Arrow, Kenneth J. 1951. *Social Choice and Individual Values.* New Haven, CT: Yale University Press.

Arrow, Kenneth J., and Gerard Debreu. 1954. "Existence of an Equilibrium for a Competitive Economy." *Econometrica* 22 (3):265–90.

Arthur, W. Brian. 1989. "Competing Technologies, Increasing Returns, and Lock-in by Historical Events." *The Economic Journal* 99:116–31.

2015. *Complexity and the Economy.* New York: Oxford University Press.

Arthur, W. Brian, Eric D. Beinhocker, and Allison Stanger, eds. 2020. *Complexity Economics: Dialogues of the Applied Complexity Network.* Kindle ed. Santa Fe: The Santa Fe Institute Press.

Atkinson, Anthony B. 2015. *Inequality: What Can Be Done?* Cambridge, MA: Harvard University Press.

Axelrod, Robert. 1984. *The Evolution of Cooperation.* New York: Basic Books.

Barabas, Chelsea, Madars Virza, Karthik Dinakar, Joichi Ito, and Jonathan Zittrain. 2018. "Interventions over Predictions: Reframing the Ethical Debate for Actuarial Risk Assessment." http://arxiv.org/abs/1712.08238.

Baran, Paul A., and Paul M. Sweezy. 1966. *Monopoly Capital: An Essay on the American Economic and Social Order.* New York: Monthly Review Press.

Barocas, Solon, and Andrew D. Selbst. 2016. "Big Data's Disparate Impact." *California Law Review* 104 (3):671–732.

Bates, Robert H. 1981. *Markets and States in Tropical Africa.* Berkeley: University of California Press.

1983. *Essays on the Political Economy of Rural Africa*. Berkeley: University of California Press.

2017. *The Development Dilemma: Security, Prosperity, and a Return to History*. Princeton, NJ: Princeton University Press.

Becker, Gary S. 1957. *The Economics of Discrimination*. Chicago: University of Chicago Press.

1964. *Human Capital*. New York: Columbia University Press.

1968. "Crime and Punishment: An Economic Approach." *Journal of Political Economy* 76:169–217.

1974. "A Theory of Marriage: Part II." *Journal of Political Economy* 2 (Mar-Apr):11-26.

Beinhocker, Eric D. 2006. *The Origin of Wealth: Evolution, Complexity, and the Radical Remaking of Economics*. Kindle ed. Boston: Harvard University Press.

Beinhocker, Eric D., and Nick Hanauer. In progress. *Market Humanism*.

Benkler, Yochai. 2002. "Coase's Penguin, or, Linux and 'The Nature of the Firm'." *The Yale Law Journal* 112 (3):369–446.

Benkler, Yochai, Aaron David Shaw, and Benjamin Mako Hill. 2015. "Peer Production: A Modality of Collective Intelligence," ed. Thomas Malone and Michael Bernstein. Cambridge, MA: MIT Press.

Beramendi, Pablo. 2012. *The Political Geography of Inequality Regions and Redistribution*. New York: Cambridge University Press.

Berlin, Isaiah. 1970. *Four Essays on Liberty*. London: Oxford University Press.

Berliner, Daniel, Anne Regan Greenleaf, Milli Lake, Margaret Levi, and Jennifer Noveck. 2015. *Labor Standards in International Supply Chains: Aligning Rights and Incentives*. Northhampton, MA: Edward Elgar.

Bernholz, Lucy, Helene Landemore, and Rob Reich, eds. 2021. *Digital Technology and Democratic Theory*. Chicago: University of Chicago Press.

Bernstein, Lisa. 1992. "Opting Out of the Legal System: Extralegal Contractual Relations in the Diamond Industry." *The Journal of Legal Studies* 21 (1):115–57.

Besley, Timothy, and Torsten Persson. 2011. *Pillars of Prosperity*. Princeton, NJ: Princeton University Press.

Block, Fred L., and Margaret R. Somers. 2014. *The Power of Market Fundamentalism: Karl Polanyi's Critique*. Cambridge, MA: Harvard University Press.

Blyth, Mark. 2002. *Great Transformations: Economic Ideas and Institutional Change in the Twentieth Century*. Cambridge: Cambridge University Press.

Boehm, Cristopher. 1999. *Hierarchy in the Forest: The Evolution of Egalitarian Behavior*. Cambridge, MA: Harvard University Press.

Boix, Carles. 1998. *Political Parties, Growth and Equality*. New York: Cambridge University Press.

2003. *Democracy and Redistribution*. New York: Cambridge University Press.

2019. *Democratic Capitalism at the Crossroads: Technological Change and the Future of Politics*. Princeton, NJ: Princeton University Press.

Booker, Cory. 2019. "Booker, Wyden, Clarke Introduce Bill Requiring Companies to Target Bias in Corporate Algorithms." http://bit.ly/3bOv4ih.

Boushey, Heather. 2019. *Unbound: How Inequality Constricts Our Economy and What We Can Do about It*. Cambridge, MA: Harvard University Press.

Bowles, Samuel. 2016. *The Moral Economy: Why Good Incentives Are No Substitute for Good Citizens*. New Haven, CT: Yale University Press.

Bowles, Samuel, and Herbert Gintis. 1977. *Schooling in Capitalist America: Educational Reform and the Contradictions of Economic Life*. New York: Basic Books.

2002. "Homo Reciprocans." *Nature* 415 (6868):125–7.

2011. *A Cooperative Species: Human Reciprocity and Its Evolution*. Princeton, NJ: Princeton University Press.

Brennan, Jason. 2016. *Against Democracy*. Princeton, NJ: Princeton University Press.

Brundage, Miles, Shahar Avin, Jasmine Wang, Haydn Belfield, Gretchen Krueger, Gillian Hadfield, Heidy Khlaaf, Jingying Yang, Helen Toner, and Ruth Fong. 2020. "Toward Trustworthy AI Development: Mechanisms for Supporting Verifiable Claims." arXivpreprinttarXiv:2004.07213.

Buchanan, James M. 1999. *The Collected Works of James M. Buchanan, Vol. 1: The Logical Foundations of Constitutional Liberty*. Indianapolis: Liberty Fund.

Buchanan, James M., and Gordon Tullock. 1965. *The Calculus of Consent: Logical Foundations of Constitutional Democracy*. Ann Arbor: University of Michigan Press.

Burgin, Angus. 2012. *The Great Persuasion: Reinventing Free Markets since the Depression*. Cambridge, MA: Harvard University Press.

Burns, Jennifer. 2018. "Review Essay of Democracy in Chains." *History of Political Economy* 50 (3):640–8.

Butler, Brian, Elisabeth Joyce, and Jacqueline Pike. 2008. "Don't Look Now, But We've Created a Bureaucracy: The Nature and Roles of Policies and Rules in Wikipedia." *Proceedings of the SIGCHI Conference on Human Factors in Computing Systems*. https://doi.org/10.1145/1357054.1357227.

Camerer, Colin, George Loewenstein, and Matthew Rabin, eds. 2004. *Advances in Behavioral Economics*. Princeton, NJ: Princeton University Press.

Camic, Charles, and Geoffrey Martin Hodgson, eds. 2011. *The Essential Writings of Thorstein Veblen*. London: Routledge.

Carlin, Wendy, and Samuel Bowles. 2020. "Shrinking Capitalism." *AEA Papers and Proceedings* 110 (May):372–7.

Carter, Zachary D. 2020. *The Price of Peace: Money, Democracy, and the Life of John Maynard Keynes*. New York: Random House.

Carugati, Federica. 2019. *Creating a Constitution: Law, Democracy, and Growth in Ancient Athens*. Princeton, NJ: Princeton University Press.

——— 2020a. "The Past and Future of Governance." Society for Institutional and Organizational Economics. www.sioe.org/news/past-and-future-governance.

——— 2020b. "Tradeoffs of Inclusion: Development in Ancient Athens." *Comparative Political Studies* 53 (1):144-70.

Carugati, Federica, Gillian K. Hadfield, and Barry R. Weingast. 2015. "Building Legal Order in Ancient Athens." *Journal of Legal Analysis* 7 (2):291–324.

Citron, Danielle Keats. 2007. "Technological Due Process." *Washington University Law Rev.* 85:1249.

Clay, Karen, and Gavin Wright. 2005. "Order without Law? Property Rights during the California Gold Rush." *Explorations in Economic History* 42 (2):155–83.

Coase, Ronald H. 1937. "The Nature of the Firm." *Economica* 4 (3):386–405.

Cohen, G. A. 2008. *Rescuing Justice and Equality*. Cambridge, MA: Harvard University Press.

Cohen, Joshua. 2001. "Money, Politics, Political Equality." In *Fact and Value*, ed. Alex Byrne, Robert Stalnaker, and Ralph Wedgewood. Cambridge, MA: MIT Press.

——— 2020. "Good Jobs." MIT Work of the Future: Research Briefs. https://workofthefuture.mit.edu/research-post/good-jobs/.

Cohen, Joshua, and Archon Fung. 2021. "Democracy and the Digital Public Sphere." In *Digital Technology and Democratic Theory*, ed. Lucy Bernholz, Helene Landemore, and Rob Reich. Chicago: University of Chicago Press.

Cohen, Joshua, and Joel Rogers, eds. 1995. *Associations and Democracy*. New York: Verso.

Collier, Paul. 2018. *The Future of Capitalism: Facing the New Anxieties*. First U.S. edition. New York: Harper.

Collier, Paul, and John Kay. 2020. *Greed is Dead*. London: Allen Lane.

Collier, Ruth Berins, and David Collier. 1991. *Shaping the Political Arena*. Princeton NJ: Princeton University Press.

Commission on the Practice of Democratic Citizenship. 2020. "Our Common Purpose: Reinventing American Democracy for the 21st century." Cambridge, MA: American Academy of Arts & Sciences.

Commons, John R. 1924. *Legal Foundations of Capitalism*. New York: Macmillan. 1934. *Institutional Economics: Its Place in Political Economy*. New York: The Macmillan Company.

Cook, Karen, Russell Hardin, and Margaret Levi. 2005. *Cooperation without Trust?* New York: Russell Sage Foundation.

Corns, Thomas N., Ann Hughes, and David Loewenstein, eds. 2009. *The Complete Works of Gerrard Winstanley*. New York: Oxford University Press.

Cottam, Hilary. 2019. *Radical Help: How We Can Remake the Relationships between Us and Revolutionise the Welfare State*. London: Virago. 2020. "Welfare 5.0: Why We Need a Social Revolution and How To Make It Happen." London: Institute for Innovation and Public Purpose..

Cottam, Hilary, and Anne-Marie Slaughter. 2020. "Covid, Care, and Connection." In progress.

Cox, Kiana. 2019. "Most U.S. Adults Feel What Happens to Their Own Racial or Ethnic Group Affects Them Personally." FactTank: Pew Research Center. www.pewresearch.org/fact-tank/2019/07/11/linked-fate-connectedness-ameri cans/.

Craig, Maureen A., and Jennifer A. Richeson. 2012. "Coalition or Derogation? How Perceived Discrimination Influences Intraminority Intergroup Relations." *Journal of Personality and Social Psychology* 102 (4):759–77.

Cramer, Katherine J. 2016. *The Politics of Resentment: Rural Consciousness in Wisconsin and the Rise of Scott Walker*. Chicago; London: University of Chicago Press.

Dahl, Robert A., and Charles E. Lindblom. 1965 [1953]. *Politics, Economics and Welfare; Planning and Politico-Economic Systems Resolved into Basic Social Processes*. New York: Harper & Row.

Darity, William A., and A. Kirsten Mullen. 2020. *From Here to Equality: Reparations for Black Americans in the Twenty-First Century*. Chapel Hill: The University of North Carolina Press.

David, Paul. 1985. "Clio and the Economics of QWERTY." *American Economic Review* 75 (2):332–7.

Dawson, Michael C. 1994. *Behind the Mule: Race and Class in African-American Politics*. Princeton, NJ: Princeton University Press.

Denzau, Arthur T., and Douglass C. North. 1994. "Shared Mental Models: Ideologies and Institutions." *Kyklos* 47 (1):3–31.

Dewey, John. 1954. *The Public and Its Problems.* Athens, Ohio: Ohio University Press.

Diamond, Jared. 2020. "The Germs that Transformed History." *Wall Street Journal,* May 22, 2020.

2012. *The World until Yesterday: What Can We Learn from Traditional Societies?* New York: Viking.

Díaz-Cayeros, Alberto, Federico Estevez, and Beatriz Magaloni. 2016. *The Political Logic of Poverty Relief: Electoral Strategies and Social Policy in Mexico.* New York: Cambridge University Press.

Downs, Anthony. 1957. *An Economic Theory of Democracy.* New York: Harper.

Edwards, J., and S. Ogilvie. 2011. "Contract Enforcement, Institutions and Social Capital: The Maghribi Traders Reappraised." 65 (2):421–44.

Edwards, Richard. 1979. *Contested Terrain: The Transformation of the Workplace in the Twentieth Century.* New York: Basic Books.

Edwards, Richard, David Gordon, and Michael Reich. 1982. *Segmented Work, Divided Workers: The Historical Transformation of Labor in the United States.* New York: Cambridge University Press.

Edwards, Richard, Michael Reich, and Thomas E. Weisskopf. 1978. *The Capitalist System: A Radical Analysis of American Society.* Englewood Cliffs, NJ: Prentice-Hall.

Ellickson, Robert C. 1991. *Order without Law: How Neighbors Settle Disputes.* Cambridge, MA: Harvard University Press.

Engstrom, David Freeman, and Daniel E Ho. 2020. "Algorithmic Accountability in the Administrative State." *Yale Journal on Regulation,* 37:800-54.

Etzioni, Oren, and Michael Li. 2019. "High-Stakes AI Decisions Need to be Automatically Audited." *Wired.* www.wired.com/story/ai-needs-to-be-audited/

Evans, Peter B., Dietrich Rueschemeyer, and Theda Skocpol. 1985. *Bringing the State Back In.* New York: Cambridge University Press.

Farrell, Henry, and Bruce Schneier. 2018. "Common-Knowledge Attacks on Democracy". Berkman Klein Center Research Publication No. 2018–7.

2019. "Democracy's Dilemma." *Boston Review.* http://bostonreview.net /forum-henry-farrell-bruce-schneier-democracys-dilemma.

Feldstein, S. 2019. "The Road to Digital Unfreedom: How Artificial Intelligence is Reshaping Repression." *Journal of Democracy* 30:40–52.

Fiske, Susan T. 2003. "Five Core Social Motives, Plus or Minus 5." In *Motivated Social Perception, The Ontario Symposium,* ed. S.J. Spencer, S. Fein, Mark P. Zanna, and J.M. Olson. Mahwah, NJ: Lawrence Erlbaum Associates Publisher.

2010. *Social Beings: Core Motives in Social Psychology*. 2nd ed. Hoboken, NJ: Wiley.

Fleischacker, Samuel. 2004. *On Adam Smith's Wealth of Nations*. Princeton, NJ: Princeton University Press.

Friedman, Milton. 1968. "The Role of Monetary Policy." *American Economic Review* 58:1–17.

Friedman, Milton, and Rose Friedman. 1980. *Free to Choose*. New York: Harcourt Brace Jovanovich.

1962. *Capitalism and Freedom*. Chicago: University of Chicago Press.

Fukuyama, Francis. 2011. *The Origins of Political Order: From Prehuman Times to the French Revolution*. New York: Farrar, Straus, and Giroux.

Fuller, Lon L. 1965. *The Morality of Law*. New Haven: Yale University Press.

Fung, Archon. 2006. *Empowered Participation: Reinventing Urban Democracy*. Princeton, NJ: Princeton University Press.

Fung, Archon, Erik Olin Wright, and Rebecca Abers. 2003. *Deepening Democracy: Institutional Innovations in Empowered Participatory Governance*. London; New York: Verso.

Galbraith, John Kenneth. 1952. *American Capitalism: The Concept Of Countervailing Power*. Boston: Houghton Mifflin.

1969. *The Affluent Society*. 2d ed. Boston: Houghton Mifflin.

1971. *The New Industrial State*. 2d ed. Boston: Houghton-Mifflin.

George, Henry, Francis K. Peddle, and William Spangar Peirce. 2016. *The Annotated Works of Henry George*. Madison, NJ: Fairleigh Dickinson University Press.

Godwin, William. 1793. *An Enquiry concerning Political Justice, and Its Influence on General Virtue and Happiness*. Dublin: Printed for L. White.

Goldberg, Jessica 2012. "Choosing and Enforcing Business Relationships in the Eleventh-Century Mediterranean: Reassessing the 'Maghribi Traders.'" *Past & Present*. 216:3-40.

González De Lara, Yadira, Avner Greif, and Saumitra Jha. 2008. "The Administrative Foundations of Self-Enforcing Constitutions." *The American Economic Review* 98 (2):105–9.

Gopnik, Alison. 2020. "Vulnerable Yet Vital: The Dance of Love and Lore between Grandparent and Grandchild Is at the Centre, Not the Fringes, of Our Evolutionary Story." *Aeon*. https://aeon.co/essays/why-childhood-and-old-age-are-key-to-our-human-capacities.

Grady, Denise. 2019. "A.I. Took a Test to Detect Lung Cancer. It Got an A." *The New York Times*. https://www.nytimes.com/2019/05/20/health/cancer-artificial-intelligence-ct-scans.html.

Green, Donald P., and Ian Shapiro. 1994. *Pathologies of Rational Choice Theory: A Critique of Applications in Political Science*. New Haven, CT: Yale University Press.

Greif, Avner. 1989. "Reputation and Coalitions in Medieval Trade: Evidence on the Maghribi Traders." *Journal of Economic History* 49 (4):857–82.

    1994. "Cultural Beliefs and the Organization of Society: A Historical and Theoretical Reflection on Collectivist and Individualist Societies." *Journal of Political Economy* 102 (5):912–50.

    2006. *Institutions and the Path to the Modern Economy: Lessons from Medieval Trade*. New York: Cambridge University Press.

Greif, Avner, and David D. Laitin. 2004. "A Theory of Endogenous Institutional Change." *American Political Science Review* 98 (4):633–52.

Hacker, Jacob S., and Paul Pierson. 2010. *Winner-Take-All-Politics*. New York: Simon & Schuster.

Hadfield, Gillian K., and Barry R. Weingast. 2012. "What Is Law? A Coordination Model of the Characteristics of Legal Order." *Journal of Legal Analysis* 4 (2):471–514.

    2013. "Law without the State: Legal Attributes and the Coordination of Decentralized Collective Punishment." *Journal of Law and Courts* 1 (1):3–34.

    2014. "Microfoundations of the Rule of Law." *Annual Review of Political Science* 17 (1):21–42.

Halfaker, Aaron, R. , Stuart Geiger, Jonathan T. Morgan, and John Riedl. 2012. "The Rise and Decline of an Open Collaboration System: How Wikipedia's Reaction to Popularity Is Causing Its Decline." *American Behavioral Scientist* 57 (5):664–88.

Hall, Peter A. 1989. *The Political Power of Economic Ideas: Keynsianism across Nations*. Princeton, NJ: Princeton University Press.

Hall, Peter A., and David Soskice, eds. 2001. *Varieties of Capitalism*. New York: Oxford University Press.

Han, Hahrie. 2014. *How Organizations Develop Activists: Civic Associations and Leadership in the 21st Century*. New York: Oxford University Press.

Handman, Max, Abbott P. Usher, George W. Stocking, V. W. Bladen, Broadus Mitchell, William Jaffee, Alvin H. Hansen, and Carter Goodrich. 1931. "Economic History – The Decline of Laissez Faire." *The American Economic Review* 21 (1):3–10.

Harari, Yuval Noah. 2018. "Why Technology Favors Tyranny." *The Atlantic* 322 (3):64-73.

Hardin, Garrett. 1968. "Tragedy of the Commons." *Science* 162 (3859):1243–8.

Hardin, Russell. 2002. *Trust and Trustworthiness*. New York: Russell Sage Foundation.

Harrington, Michael. 1962. *The Other America: Poverty in the United States*. New York: Macmillan.

Hayek, Friedrich A. von. 1944. *The Road to Serfdom*. London: G. Routledge & Sons.

——— 1960. *The Constitution of Liberty*. Chicago: University of Chicago Press.

——— 1974. "The Pretense of Knowledge." Prize Lecture. Nobelprize.org. www .nobelprize.org/prizes/economic-sciences/1974/hayek/lecture/.

Henderson, Rebecca. 2020. *Reimagining Capitalism in a World on Fire*. New York: Public Affairs.

Hirschman, Albert O. 1977. *The Passions and the Interests: Political Arguments for Capitalism before Its Triumph*. Princeton, NJ: Princeton University Press.

Hochschild, Arlie Russell. 2016. *Strangers in Their Own Land: Anger and Mourning on the American Right*. New York: New Press.

Hovenkamp, Herbert. 2009. "United States Competition Policy in Crisis: 1890–1955." *Minnesota Law Review* 94 (311):311–67.

Hume, David. 1975. *Enquiries concerning Human Understanding and concerning the Principles of Morals*. 3rd ed. Oxford: Clarendon Press.

Iversen, Torben. 1999. *Contested Economic Institutions: The Politics of Macroeconomics and Wage Bargaining in Advanced Democracies*. New York: Cambridge University Press.

——— 2005. *Capitalism, Democracy, and Welfare*. New York: Cambridge University Press.

Iversen, Torben, and David Soskice. 2019. *Democracy and Prosperity: Reinventing Capitalism through a Turbulent Century*. Princeton, NJ: Princeton University Press.

Jackson, Matthew O. 2008. *Social and Economic Networks*. Princeton, NJ: Princeton University Press.

——— 2019. *The Human Network: How Your Social Position Determines Your Power, Beliefs, and Behaviors*. New York: Pantheon Books.

Jacobs, Michael, and Mariana Mazzucato, eds. 2016. *Rethinking Capitalism*. Oxford: Wiley-Blackwell.

Janeway, William H. 2020. "The Master and the Prodigy." Project Syndicate. www.project-syndicate.org/onpoint/review-frank-ramsey-keynes-price-of -peace-by-william-h-janeway-2020-08?barrier=accesspaylog.

Jevons, William Stanley. 1965 [1888]. *The Theory of Political Economy*. 5th ed. New York: A. M. Kelley.

Kadens, E. 2015. "The Medieval Law Merchant: The Tyranny of a Construct." *Journal of Legal Analysis* 7 (2):251-89.

Kahneman, Daniel. 2011. *Thinking, Fast and Slow.* New York: Farrar, Straus, and Giroux.

Kalyvas, Andreas, and Ira Katznelson. 2008. *Liberal Beginnings: Making a Republic for the Moderns.* Cambridge: Cambridge University Press.

Keynes, John Maynard. 1926. *The End of Laissez-Faire.* London: L. & Virginia Woolf.

   1932. *Essays in Persuasion.* New York: Harcourt, Brace and Co.

   1936. *The General Theory of Employment, Interest and Money.* New York: Harcourt, Brace.

   1937. "The General Theory of Unemployment." *The Quarterly Journal of Economics* 51 (2):209–23.

King, Martin Luther, Jr. 1964. *Why We Can't Wait.* New York: Harper and Row.

Kinzig, Ann P., Paul R. Ehrlich, Lee J. Alston, Kenneth Arrow, Scott Barrett, Timothy G. Buchman, Gretchen C. Daily, Bruce Levin, Simon Levin, Michael Oppenheimer, Elinor Ostrom, and Donald Saari. 2013. "Social Norms and Global Environmental Challenges: The Complex Interaction of Behaviors, Values, and Policy." *BioScience* 63 (3):164–75.

Kitschelt, Herbert, and Steven Wilkinson. 2007. *Patrons, Clients, and Policies: Patterns of Democratic Accountability and Political Competition.* New York: Cambridge University Press.

Kittur, Aniket, Ed Chi, Bryan A. Pendleton, Bongwon Suh, and Todd Mytkowicz. 2007. "Power of the Few vs. Wisdom of the Crowd: Wikipedia and the Rise of the Bourgeoisie." *CHI '07: Proceedings of the SIGCHI Conference on Human Factors in Computing Systems* 1 (2):19.

Kittur, Aniket, and Robert E. Kraut. 2010. "Beyond Wikipedia: Coordination and Conflict in Online Production Groups." ACM Digital Library. https://dl.acm.org/doi/10.1145/1718918.1718959.

Kleinberg, Jon, Jens Ludwig, Sendhil Mullainathan, and Cass R. Sunstein. 2018. "Discrimination in the Age of Algorithms." *Journal of Legal Analysis* 10:113–74.

Klinenberg, Eric. 2018. *Palaces for the People: How Social Infrastructure Can Help Fight Inequality, Polarization, and the Decline of Civic Life.* New York: Crown.

Knight, Jack, and James Johnson. 2011. *The Priority of Democracy: A Pragmatist Argument.* Princeton, NJ: Princeton University Press / Russell Sage Foundation Press.

Kundanini, Hans. 2018. "Lost in Translation: Communities of Fate." *Berlin Policy Journal*. https://berlinpolicyjournal.com/lost-in-translation-communities-of-fate/.

Kuran, Timur. 1995. *Private Truths, Public Lies*. Cambridge, MA: Harvard University Press.

Landemore, Hélène. 2013. *Democratic Reason: Politics, Collective Intelligence, and the Rule of the Many*. Princeton, NJ: Princeton University Press.

Landemore, Hélène, and Jon Elster. 2012. *Collective Wisdom: Principles and Mechanisms*. New York: Cambridge University Press.

Letwin, William. 1981. *Law and Economic Policy in America: The Evolution of the Sherman Antitrust Act*. Phoenix ed. Chicago: University of Chicago Press.

Levi, Margaret. 1981. "The Predatory Theory of Rule." *Politics & Society* 10 (4):431–65.

1988. *Of Rule and Revenue*. Berkeley: The University of California Press.

1997. *Consent, Dissent and Patriotism*. New York: Cambridge University Press.

2019. "Trustworthy Government, Legitimating Beliefs." In *Political Legitimacy NOMOS: LXI*, ed. Jack Knight and Melissa Schwartzberg. New York: New York University Press.

2020. "An Expanded Community of Fate." *Noema*. Los Angeles: Berggruen Institute.

Levi, Margaret, Tania Melo, Barry Weingast, and Frances Zlotnick. 2017. "Opening Access, Ending the Violence Trap: Labor, Business, Government, and the National Labor Relations Act." In *Organizations, Civil Society, and the Roots of Development*, ed. Naomi R. Lamoreaux and John Wallis. Chicago: University of Chicago Press.

Levi, Margaret, and Laura Stoker. 2000. "Political Trust and Trustworthiness." *Annual Review of Political Science* 3:475–507.

Liu, Glory M, and Barry Weingast. Forthcoming. "Deriving 'General Principles': Adam Smith's Pervasive Use of Equilibrium and Comparative Statics Analysis." *Adam Smith Review*.

Mackie, Gerry. 2009. "Schumpeter's Leadership Democracy." *Political Theory* 37 (1):128–53.

MacLean, Nancy. 2017. *Democracy in Chains: The Deep History of the Radical Right's Stealth Plan for America*. New York: Viking.

Malthus, Thomas R. 1986. *The Works of Thomas Robert Malthus*. ed. E. A. Wrigley and David Souden. London: Pickering.

Mann, Geoff. 2017. *In the Long Run We Are All Dead: Keynesianism, Political Economy, and Revolution*. Kindle ed. London: Verso.

Mares, Isabela. 2003. *The Politics of Social Risk: Business and Welfare State Development*. New York: Cambridge University Press.

2006. *Taxation, Wage Bargaining, and Unemployment*. New York: Cambridge.

Marglin, Stephen A. 1974. "What Do Bosses Do? The Origins and Functions of Hierarchy in Capitalist Production, Part I." *The Review of Radical Political Economics* 6 (2):60–112.

1975. "What Do Bosses Do? The Origins and Functions of Hierarchy in Capitalist Production, Part II." *The Review of Radical Political Economics* 7 (1):20–37.

Marshall, Alfred. 1936 [1920]. *Principles of Economics: An Introductory Volume*. 8th ed. London: Macmillan.

Marx, Karl. 1974 [1867]. *Capital*. Vol. I. First English ed. of 1887. New York: International Publishers.

Marx, Karl, and Friedrich Engels. 1978 [1848]. *Manifesto of the Communist Party*. 2nd ed., ed. Robert C. Tucker. New York: W.W. Norton.

Mayer, Colin P. 2018. *Prosperity: Better Business Makes the Greater Good*. First ed. Oxford: Oxford University Press.

Mayson, Sandra G. 2019. "Bias in, Bias out." *Yale Law Journal* 128 (8):2218–300.

Mazzucato, Mariana. 2018. *The Value of Everything: Making and Taking in the Global Economy*. First US ed. New York: Public Affairs.

Milgrom, Paul R., Douglas C. North, and Barry R. Weingast. 1990. "The Role of Institutions in the Revival of Trade: The Medieval Law Merchant, Private Judges, and the Champagne Fairs." *Economics and Politics* 2 (1):1–23.

Mill, James. 1844 [1821]. *Elements of Political Economy*. London: Henry G. Bohn.

Mill, John Stuart. 1882. *Considerations on Representative Government*. New York: H. Holt.

Mitchell, William C. 1984. "Schumpeter and Public Choice, Part II: Democracy and the Demise of Capitalism: The Missing Chapter in Schumpeter." *Public Choice* 42 (2):161–74.

Mittal, Sonia, and Barry R. Weingast. 2013. "Self-Enforcing Constitutions: With an Application to Democratic Stability in America's First Century." *The Journal of Law, Economics, and Organization* 29 (2):278–302.

Moe, Terry. 2005. "Power and Political Institutions." *Perspectives on Politics* 3 (2):215–33.

Morris, Ian, Richard Seaford, and Stephen Macedo. 2015. *Foragers, Farmers, and Fossil Fuels: How Human Values Evolve*. Princeton, NJ: Princeton University Press.

Narayan, Sneha, Nathan TeBlunthuis, Wm Salt Hale, Benjamin Mako Hill, and Aaron Shaw. 2019. "All Talk: How Increasing Interpersonal Communication on Wikis May Not Enhance Productivity." *Proc. ACM Human-Computer Interaction* 3 (CSCW). https://doi.org/10.1145/3359203.

North, Douglass C. 1981. *Structure and Change in Economic History.* New York: Norton.

———. 1990. *Institutions, Institutional Change, and Economic Performance.* New York: Cambridge University Press.

North, Douglass C., John Wallis, and Barry Weingast. 2009. *Violence and Social Orders: A Conceptual Framework for Interpreting Recorded Human History.* New York: Cambridge University Press.

North, Douglass C., and Barry R. Weingast. 1989. "Constitutions and Commitment: The Evolution of Institutions Governing Public Choice in Seventeenth Century England." *Journal of Economic History* 49 (4):803–32.

Nussbaum, Martha. 2011. *Creating Capabilities: The Human Development Approach.* Cambridge, MA: Harvard University Press.

Obama, Barack. 2020. *A Promised Land.* First ed. New York: Crown.

Ober, Josiah. 2008. *Democracy and Knowledge: Innovation and Learning in Classical Athens.* Princeton, NJ: Princeton University Press.

———. 2012. "Democracy's Dignity." *American Political Science Review* 106 (4): 827–46. https://doi.org/10.1017/S000305541200038X.

———. 2015. *The Rise and Fall of Classical Greece.* Princeton, NJ: Princeton University Press.

Oguz, Fuat. 2010. "Hayek on Tacit Knowledge." *Journal of Institutional Economics* 6 (2):145–65.

Olson, Mancur. 1965. *The Logic of Collective Action.* Cambridge, MA: Harvard University Press.

———. 1982. *The Rise and Decline of Nations.* New Haven, CT: Yale University Press.

Ostrom, Elinor. 1990. *Governing the Commons: The Evolution of Institutions for Collective Action.* New York: Cambridge University Press.

———. 2010a. "Beyond Markets and States: Polycentric Governance of Complex Economic Systems." *American Economic Review* 100:641–72.

———. 2010b. "An Interview with Elinor Ostrom," interview by Margaret Levi. Annual Reviews Conversations. www.annualreviews.org/userimages/contenteditor/1326999553977/elinorostromtranscript.pdf.

2010c. "A Long Polycentric Journey." *Annual Review of Political Science* 13:1–23.

Page, Benjamin I., and Martin Gilens. 2017. *Democracy in America? What Has Gone Wrong and What We Can Do about It.* Chicago: University of Chicago Press.

Papageorgiou, Theofanis, Ioannis Katselidis, and Panayotis G. Michaelides. 2013. "Schumpeter, Commons, and Veblen on Institutions." *The American Journal of Economics and Sociology* 72 (5):1232–54.

Pareto, Vilfredo. 2013 [1906]. *Manual of Political Economy: A Variorum Translation and Critical Edition.* Oxford: Oxford University Press.

Parijs, Philippe van. 1995. *Real Freedom for All: What (If Anything) Can Justify Capitalism?* Oxford: Clarendon Press.

Parijs, Philippe van, and Yannick Vanderborght. 2017. *Basic Income: A Radical Proposal for a Free Society and a Sane Economy.* Cambridge, MA: Harvard University Press.

Paul, Mark, William A. Darity, and Darrick Hamilton. 2018. *The Federal Job Guarantee – A Policy to Achieve Permanent Full Employment.* Washington, DC: Center of Budget and Policy Priorities.

Pendleton-Jullian, Ann, and John Seely Brown. 2018. *Design Unbound*, Vols. 1 and 2. Cambridge, MA: MIT.

Pettit, Philip. 2014. *Just Freedom: A Moral Compass for a Complex World.* First ed. New York: W.W. Norton & Company.

Phillips-Fein, Kim. 2009. *Invisible Hands: The Businessmen's Crusade against the New Deal.* New York: W. W. Norton.

Philp, Mark. 2017. "William Godwin." In *The Stanford Encyclopedia of Philosophy.* https://plato.stanford.edu/entries/godwin/.

Pierson, Paul. 2004. *Politics in Time: History, Institutions, and Social Analysis.* Princeton, NJ: Princeton University Press.

Piketty, Thomas. 2014. *Capital in the Twenty-First Century.* tr. Arthur Goldhammer. Cambridge MA: Belknap Press of Harvard University Press.

2020. *Capital and Ideology.* Cambridge, MA: Belknap Press of Harvard University Press.

Polanyi, Karl. 1957. *The Great Transformation.* Boston: Beacon Press.

Posner, Eric A., and Glen Weyl. 2018. *Radical Markets: Uprooting Capitalism and Democracy for a Just Society.* Princeton, NJ: Princeton University Press.

Przeworski, Adam. 1985. *Capitalism and Social Democracy.* New York: Cambridge University Press.

1999. "Minimalist Conception of Democracy: A Defense." In *Democracy's Value*, ed. Ian Shapiro and Casiano Hacker-Cordon. New York: Cambridge University Press.

Przeworski, Adam, and John Sprague. 1986. *Paper Stones: A History of Electoral Socialism*. New York: Cambridge University Press.

Przeworski, Adam, and Michael Wallerstein. 1982. "The Structure of Class Conflict in Democratic Capitalist Societies." *American Political Science Review* 76 (2):215–38.

1988. "Structural Dependence of the State on Capital." *American Political Science Review* 82:11–30.

Putnam, Robert D. 1993. *Making Democracy Work: Civic Traditions in Modern Italy*. Princeton, NJ: Princeton University Press.

2000. *Bowling Alone: The Collapse and Revival of American Community*. New York: Simon & Schuster.

Putnam, Robert D., and Shaylyn Romney Garrett. 2020. *The Upswing: How America Came Together a Century Ago and How We Can Do It Again*. New York: Simon & Schuster.

Rahman, Kazi Sabeel, and Hollie Russon Gilman. 2019. *Civic Power: Rebuilding American Democracy in an Era of Crisis*. New York: Cambridge University Press.

Raji, Inioluwa Deborah, Andrew Smart, Rebecca N. White, Margaret Mitchell, Timnit Gebru, Ben Hutchinson, Jamila Smith-Loud, Daniel Theron, and Parker Barnes. 2020. "Closing the AI Accountability Gap: Defining an End-To-End Framework for Internal Algorithmic Auditing." https://arxiv.org/pdf/2001.00973.pdf.

Rawls, John. 1971. *A Theory of Justice*. Cambridge, MA: Harvard University Press.

1993. *Political Liberalism*. New York: Columbia University Press.

Raworth, Kate. 2017. *Doughnut Economics: Seven Ways to Think Like a 21st Century Economist*. White River Junction, VT: Chelsea Green Publishing.

Reisman, Dillon, Jason Schultz, Kate Crawford, and Meredith Whittaker. 2018. "Algorithmic Impact Assessments: A Practical Framework for Public Agency Accountability." AI Now Institute. https://ainowinstitute.org/aiareport2018.pdf.

Rhodes, Ben. 2019. *The World as It Is*. New York: Random House.

Ricardo, David. 2001 [1817]. *On the Principles of Political Economy and Taxation*. London: Electric Book Co.

Richman, Barak. 2017. *Stateless Commerce: The Diamond Network and the Persistence of Relational Exchange*. Cambridge, MA: Harvard University Press.

Riker, William H. 1962. *The Theory of Political Coalitions*. New Haven, CT: Yale University Press.

1964. *Federalism*. Boston: Little, Brown.

1984. "The Heresthetics of Constitution-Making: The Presidency in 1787, with Comments on Determinism and Rational Choice." *American Political Science Review* 78 (1):1–16.

Robinson, Joan. 1969. *The Accumulation of Capital*. 3rd ed. London: Macmillan.

1979. *Collected Economic Papers*, Vol. 5. Oxford: Basil Blackwell.

Rodrik, Dani. 2015. *Economics Rules: The Rights and Wrongs of the Dismal Science*. First ed. New York: W.W. Norton & Company.

Roemer, John. 1982. *A General Theory of Exploitation and Class*. Cambridge, MA: Harvard University Press.

1988. *Free to Lose: An Introduction to Marxist Economic Philosophy*. Cambridge, MA: Harvard University Press.

Rogan, Tim. 2017. *The Moral Economists: R. H. Tawney, Karl Polanyi, E. P. Thompson, and the Critique of Capitalism*. Princeton, NJ: Princeton University Press.

Rothschild, Michael, and Joseph Stiglitz. 1976. "Equilibrium in Competitive Insurance Markets: An Essay on the Economics of Imperfect Information." *The Quarterly Journal of Economics* 90 (4):629–49.

Sabel, Charles F. 2012. "Dewey, Democracy, and Democratic Experimentalism." *Contemporary Pragmatism* 9 (2):35–55.

Samuelson, Paul A. 1938. "A Note on the Pure Theory of Consumer's Behaviour." *Economica* 5 (17):61–71.

Samuelson, Paul, and William Nordhaus. 1998. *Economics*. 16th edition. Boston: Irwin/McGraw-Hill.

Sandel, Michael J. 2012. *What Money Can't Buy: The Moral Limits of Markets*. New York: Farrar, Straus and Giroux.

2020. *The Tyranny of Merit: What's Become of the Common Good?* New York: Farrar, Straus & Giroux.

Satz, Deborah. 2010. *Why Some Things Should Not be for Sale: The Moral Limits of Markets*. New York: Oxford University Press.

Satz, Deborah, and Stuart White. Forthcoming. "What Is Wrong with Inequality," being prepared for *Inequality: The IFS Deaton Review*. https://www.ifs.org.uk/inequality/themes/whats-wrong-with-inequality/.

Say, Jean-Baptiste. 1834 [1803]. *A Treatise on Political Economy*. Translated by C.R. Prinsep. 6th American ed. Philadelphia: Grigg & Elliott.

Scanlon, Thomas M. 2018. *Why Does Inequality Matter?* Oxford: Oxford University Press.

Scheidel, Walter. 2017. *The Great Leveler: Violence and the History of Inequality from the Stone Age to the Twenty-First Century*. Princeton, NJ: Princeton University Press.

Scheve, Kenneth, and David Stasavage. 2009. "Institutions, Partisanship, and Inequality in the Long Run." *World Politics* 61 (02).

Schneider, Nathan. 2019. "Admins, Mods, and Benevolent Dictators for Life: The Implicit Feudalism of Online Communities."*New Media & Society.* https://doi.org/10.1177/1461444820986553.

Schofield, Norman. 2006. *Architects of Political Change: Constitutional Quandaries and Social Choice Theory.* Cambridge: Cambridge University Press.

Schumpeter, Joseph A. 1942. *Capitalism, Socialism, and Democracy.* New York: Harper and Brothers.

Scott, James C. 1985. *Weapons of the Weak.* New Haven, CT: Yale University Press.

Selbst, Andrew D. 2017. "Disparate Impact in Big Data Policing." *Georgia Law Review.* 52 (109) http://dx.doi.org/10.2139/ssrn.2819182.

Sen, Amartya. 1989. "Development as Capability Expansion." *Journal of Development Planning* 19:41–58.

1999. *Development as Freedom.* New York: Oxford University Press.

Sen, Amartya K. 1977. "Rational Fools." *Philosophy and Public Affairs* 6 (4):317–44.

Sgueo, Gianluca. 2020. "The Practice of Democracy: A Selection of Civic Engagement Initiatives" EPRS, European Parliament, 2020.

Shaw, Aaron, and Benjamin M. Hill. 2014. "Laboratories of Oligarchy? How the Iron Law Extends to Peer Production." *Journal of Communication* 64 (2):215–38.

Simien, Evelyn M. 2005. "Race, Gender, and Linked Fate." *Journal of Black Studies* 35 (5):529–50.

Simon, Herbert A. 1947. *Administrative Behavior.* New York: MacMillan.

1982. *Models of Bounded Rationality: Empirically Grounded Economic Reason.* Vol. 3. Cambridge, MA: MIT Press.

Simonton, Matthew. 2019. *Classical Greek Oligarchy: A Political History.* Princeton, NJ: Oxford University Press.

Skidelsky, Robert. 1994. *John Maynard Keynes: Vol. 2: The Economist as Saviour, 1920–1937.* New York: Penguin Books.

Skocpol, Theda. 2003. *Diminished Democracy: From Membership to Management in American Civic Life.* Norman: University of Oklahoma Press.

Slaughter, Anne-Marie. 2017. *The Chessboard & the Web: Strategies of Connection in a Networked World.* New Haven, CT: Yale University Press.

Slobodian, Quinn. 2020. *Globalists: The End of Empire and the Birth of Neoliberalism.* Cambridge, MA: Harvard University Press.

Smith, Adam. 1982 [1759]. *The Theory of Moral Sentiments*. Indianapolis, IN: Liberty Fund.

———. 1986 [1776]. *An Inquiry into the Nature and Causes of the Wealth of Nations*. Harmondsworth, Middlesex, UK: Penguin Books.

Smith, Vernon L. 2012. "Adam Smith on Humanomic Behavior." *The Journal of Behavioral Finance & Economics*. 2(1):1–20.

Smith, Vernon L., and Bart J. Wilson. 2019. *Humanomics: Moral Sentiments and the Wealth of Nations for the Twenty-First Century*. New York: Cambridge University Press.

Stasavage, David. 2011. *States of Credit: Size, Power, and the Development of European Polities*. Princeton, NJ: Princeton University Press.

———. 2020. *The Decline and Rise of Democracy: A Global History from Antiquity to Today*. Princeton, NJ: Princeton University Press.

Steinberg, Jessica, Cyanne L. Loyle, and Federica Carugati. 2021. "Domestic Digital Repression and Cyber Peace." In Scott J. Schackleford, Frederick Duzet, and Chris Anderson, eds. *Cyber Peace: Charting a Path toward a Sustainable and Secure Cyberspace*. New York: Cambridge University Press.

Stigler, George J. 1971. "The Theory of Economic Regulation." *The Bell Journal of Economics and Management Science* 2 (1):3–21.

Stigler, George J., and Gary Becker. 1977. "De Gustibus Non Est Disputandum." *American Economic Review* 67 (2):76–90.

Stiglitz, Joseph E. 1977. "Monopoly, Non-Linear Pricing and Imperfect Information: The Insurance Market." *The Review of Economic Studies* 44 (3):407–30.

Streeck, Wolfgang. 2016. *How Will Capitalism End? Essays on a Failing System*. London: Verso.

Sunstein, Cass R. 2019. "Algorithms, Correcting Biases." *Social Research: An International Quarterly* 86 (2):499–511.

TeBlunthuis, Nathan, Aaron Shaw, and Benjamin Mako Hill. 2018. "Revisiting 'The Rise and Decline' in a Population of Peer Production Projects." https://doi.org/10.1145/3173574.3173929.

Teegarden, David Arlo. 2014. *Death to Tyrants! Ancient Greek Democracy and the Struggle against Tyranny*. Princeton, NJ: Princeton University Press.

Teles, Steven Michael. 2008. *The Rise of the Conservative Legal Movement: The Battle for Control of the Law*. Princeton, NJ: Princeton University Press.

Thaler, Richard H., ed. 1991. *Quasi-Rational Economics*. New York: Russell Sage Foundation.

Thaler, Richard H., and Cass R. Sunstein. 2008. *Nudge: Improving Decisions about Health, Wealth, and Happiness*. New Haven, CT.: Yale University Press.

Thelen, Kathleen. 1999. "Historical Institutionalism in Comparative Politics." *Annual Review of Political Science* 2:369–404.

2004. *How Institutions Evolve the Political Economy of Skills in Germany, Britain, the United States, and Japan.* Cambridge: Cambridge University Press.

Forthcoming. "Employer Organization in the United States: Historical Legacies and the Long Shadow of the American Courts." Washington, DC: Economic Policy Institute.

Thelen, Kathleen, and Sven Steinmo. 1992. "Historical Institutionalism in Comparative Perspective." In *Structuring Politics*, ed. Sven Steinmo, Kathleen Thelan and Frank Longstreth. New York: Cambridge University Press.

Thompson, Derek. 2013. "Why Economics Is Really Called 'the Dismal Science': The (Not-So-Dismal) Origin Myth of a Ubiquitous Term." *The Atlantic.*

Thucydides. 2013. "The War of the Peloponnesians and the Athenians." Cambridge: Cambridge University Press.

Thurston, Chloe N. 2018. *At the Boundaries of Homeownership: Credit, Discrimination, and the American State.* New York: Cambridge University Press.

Tocqueville, Alexis de. 1990 [1835]. *Democracy in America.* Vol. I. New York: Vintage.

United States. Congress. Senate. Committee on the Judiciary. 1990. *Women and Violence: Hearing before the Committee on the Judiciary, United States Senate, One Hundred First Congress, Second Session, on Legislation to Reduce the Growing Problem of Violent Crime against Women, June 20, 1990.* Washington: US Government Printing Office.

Veblen, Thorstein. 1898. "Why is Economics Not an Evolutionary Science?" *Quarterly Journal of Economics* 12 (4 [July]):373–97.

1953 [1912]. *The Theory of the Leisure Class; An Economic Study of Institutions.* New York: New American Library.

1914. *The Instinct of Workmanship, and the State of the Industrial Arts.* New York: Macmillan.

Walras, Léon. 2013 [1889]. *Elements of Pure Economics.* Hoboken, NJ: Taylor and Francis.

Ward, Jacob. 2020. "Hacking Your Mind." 4 episodes. Directed by Carl Byker, written by Carl Byker and Jacob Ward, featuring Jacob Ward. Aired September 1, 9, 16, and 23 on PBS. https://www.pbs.org/show/hacking-your-mind/.

Ward, Michael D., Katherine Stovel, and Audrey Sacks. 2011. "Network Analysis and Political Science." *Annual Review of Political Science* 14 (1):245–64.

Weingast, Barry R. 2017. "Adam Smith's Theory of Violence and the Political Economics of Development." In *Organizations, Civil Society, and the Roots of Development*, ed. Naomi R. Lamoreaux and John Wallis. Chicago: University of Chicago.

———. 1995. "The Economic Role of Political Institutions: Market-Preserving Federalism and Economic Development." *Journal of Law, Economics, and Organization* 11 (Spring):1–31.

———. 1997. "The Political Foundations of Democracy and the Rule of Law." *American Political Science Review* 91 (2):245–63.

———. 2005. "Persuasion, Preference Change, and Critical Junctures: The Microfoundations of a Macroscopic Concept." In *Preferences and Situations*, ed. Ira Katznelson and Barry Weingast. New York: Russell Sage Foundation.

Weir, Margaret. 1989. "Ideas and Politics: The Acceptance of Keynsianism in Britain and the United States." In *The Political Power of Economic Ideas: Keynsianism across Nations*, ed. Peter A. Hall. Princeton, NJ: Princeton University Press.

Woodly, Deva R. 2015. *The Politics of Common Sense: How Social Movements Use Public Discourse to Change Politics and Win Acceptance*. New York: Oxford University Press.

Wright, Erik Olin. 2010. *Envisioning Real Utopias*. New York: Verso

Acknowledgements

In early 2018, Margaret met with the president of the Hewlett Foundation, Larry Kramer, to pitch a proposal for how to generate the thinking necessary to construct an alternative political economy. He, in turn, shared his concerns about the future of capitalist democracies and his draft formulation of a new Hewlett special project, "Beyond Neoliberalism." Funding from this project has been pivotal in developing the program Margaret and Federica ran together at the Center for Advanced Study in the Behavioral Sciences (CASBS) from the summer of 2018 to the summer of 2020. This Element is one result of that ongoing endeavor.

Despite its somewhat dense title, the program "Creating the Framework for a New Moral Political Economy" has given us tremendous enthusiasm, some hope, fresh ideas, and a large network of friends, collaborators, and colleagues working cooperatively to bring about change and reform of our current political and economic structures. Our network includes more than one hundred academics, technologists, civil society activists, policymakers, writers, and journalists. Through large meetings and small working groups, offline and online gatherings, the writing of papers and op-eds, the network shaped our path and our ideas. Naming everyone would take up a good chunk of our word allotment. But a few of them deserve a special thanks for helping us get off the ground and for running parts of the project. These are John Ahlquist, Jenna Bednar, Heather Boushey, John Seely Brown, Angus Burgin, Henry Farrell, Marion Fourcade, Jack Knight, John Markoff, Kim Stanley Robinson, Paul Saffo, Debra Satz, Lily Tsai, and Leif Wenar. We also want to express our appreciation of the outstanding CASBS staff who make our work and lives easier in innumerable ways. In addition, we are grateful to our wonderful undergraduate research assistants, Isaac Arocha, Mila Camargo, Sean Chen, Nathan Lee, Sun Lee, and Matthew Zheng, supported by Stanford's Summer Research College and the Stanford King Center on Global Development.

The crisis of democracy that is still unfolding had a silver lining for us. As we worked on the project and broadened our network, we encountered so many other people and groups concerned with similar issues. They helped us become more knowledgeable about both the problems and the range of possible solutions. For sharing their work, insights, and expertise with us, we thank Danielle Allen, Yochai Benkler and Rebecca Henderson (Political Economy and Justice); Eric Beinhocker (Institute for New Economic Thinking, Oxford); Sam Bowles and Wendy Carlin (CORE); Hilary Cottam (Participle); Yakov Feygin and Nils Gilman (Berggruen Institute); Elizabeth Garlow, Tara McGuinness, and

Anne-Marie Slaughter (New America); Chris Field and Jim Leape (Woods Institute, Stanford); Antara Haldar (Future of Economics, Cambridge University); Nick Hanauer (Civic Ventures); Mike Konczal (Rockefeller Institute); Maribel Morey (International Political Economy); Amy Kapczynski (Law and Political Economy); Jennifer Harris and Larry Kramer (Hewlett Foundation); William Janeway and Pia Malaney (Institute for New Economic Thinking); Colin Mayer (British Academy, Future of the Corporation); Sabeel Rahman (Demos); Dani Rodrik, Suresh Naidu and Gabriel Zucman (Economics for Inclusive Prosperity); Steve Teles (Niskanen Institute); Kathleen Thelen, Paul Pierson, and Alex Hertel-Fernandez, (American Political Economy); Dorian Warren (Center for Community Change); and Glen Weyl (Radical Exchange). Other participants in our workshops and seminars also contributed to our thinking. Our list of names is not fully inclusive, but we do want to note the influence of Sonja Amadae, Binyamin Appelbaum, Chris Benner, Michael Brownstein, Paul Collier, William Darrity, Darrick Hamilton, Michael Hiscox, Louis Hyman, Natasha Iskander, Dan Kelly, Stephen Macekura, Margaret O'Mara, Brandon Terry, Manuel Pastor, Prerna Singh, Chloe Thurston, Maya Tudor, and Deva Woodly.

Several people gave us comments on drafts of the Element. We are grateful to John Ahlquist, Paul Brest, John Seely Brown, David Chilosi, Roberta Katz, Larry Kramer, William Janeway, John Irons, Anne-Marie Slaughter, Kathleen Thelen, Barry Weingast, and two anonymous reviewers. We acknowledge with special gratitude the editor of the series, David Stasavage. All caught and helped us correct weaknesses in the earlier drafts and offered extraordinarily useful suggestions for improvement.

Last but not least, we would like to express our gratitude to our generous funders, the Hewlett Foundation and Reid Hoffman, as well as the Ford Foundation and Berggruen Institute for additional support.

Cambridge Elements ☰

Political Economy

David Stasavage
New York University

David Stasavage is Julius Silver Professor in the Wilf Family Department of Politics at New York University. He previously held positions at the London School of Economics and at Oxford University. His work has spanned a number of different fields and currently focuses on two areas: development of state institutions over the long run and the politics of inequality. He is a member of the American Academy of Arts and Sciences.

About the Series

The Element Series Political Economy provides authoritative contributions on important topics in the rapidly growing field of political economy. Elements are designed so as to provide broad and in depth coverage combined with original insights from scholars in political science, economics, and economic history. Contributions are welcome on any topic within this field.

Cambridge Elements $\equiv$

Political Economy

Elements in the Series

Wyt ti'n
gwybod

C000110204

Llyfr teithio Noa

www.peniarth.cymru

Testun: Non ap Emlyn, 2018
© Delweddau: Canolfan Peniarth, Prifysgol Cymru Y Drindod Dewi Sant, 2018

Golygyddion: Lowri Lloyd ac Eleri Jenkins

Dyluniwyd gan Sian Elin Evans

© Lluniau: Shutterstock.com. t.2 Jeffrey Blackler / Alamy Stock Photo. t.3Holger Burmeister /
Alamy Stock Photo. t.3 Alex Ramsay / Alamy Stock Photo. t.3 Tony Smith / Alamy Stock Photo.
t.5 Chris Hellier / Alamy Stock Photo. t.5 Gabbro / Alamy Stock Photo. t.6 a-plus image bank
/ Alamy Stock Photo. t.6 Graham Prentice / Alamy Stock Photo. t.7 dov makabaw sundry
/ Alamy Stock Photo. t.7 Adrian Grabowski / Alamy Stock Photo. t.9 Melvyn Longhurst /
Alamy Stock Photo. t.9 Eddie Gerald / Alamy Stock Photo. t.11 Wiskerke / Alamy Stock Photo.
t.11 incredible india travel stock images / Alamy Stock Photo

Cyhoeddwyd yn 2018 gan Ganolfan Peniarth

Wyt ti'n gwybod

Cynnwys

Beic

beic

beic mynydd

beic isel

beic fel car

beic saith person

beic tacsi

Gwahanol iawn!

Car

hen
gar

car
cyflym

car fel
esgid

car
diddorol

Bobl bach!

Bws

bws lliwgar

bws llawn

bws arbennig, bws ar y ffordd a ...

... bws yn y dŵr

Mawredd mawr!

Teithio ar gefn...

ceffyl

eliffant

camel

asyn

Anifeiliaid yn tynnu

ceffyl yn
tynnu cart

camel yn
tynnu cart

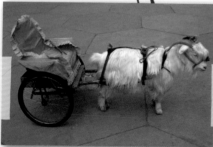

gafr yn
tynnu cart

Nefi wen!

Cwch

cwch camlas

Lliwgar!

cwch hwylio

cwch cyflym

cychod gwahanol

Nefi bliw!

Yn yr awyr

awyren

hofrennydd

parasiwt

balŵn aer poeth

Hyfryd!

Mynegai